ORDEAL *IN* ROMFORD

2/6 NET *Proceeds to Local Charities*

ORDEAL IN ROMFORD

Edited by
GLYN RICHARDS

IAN HENRY PUBLICATIONS

Originally published in 1945
This edition © Havering Museum, Ltd. 2005

ISBN 0 86025 923 4

Published by
Ian Henry Publications, Ltd.
20 Park Drive, Romford, Essex RM1 4LH
and printed by
L.P.P.S. Ltd.

NEW FOREWORD

This book telling of Romford's 'incidents' in the Second World War was published in November, 1945 (price 2/6d [12½ pence]) by the Mutual Help Association. It is here reprinted, but with the addition of an index, a map and with the photographs distributed around the text.

The original edition had its proceeds dedicated to eleven charities, many of which no longer exist, so the royalties from this printing are to be given to a single charity that seeks to bring the past of the Borough to life – Havering Museum, Ltd., to which the copyright for the format and index have been assigned.

This reprint is taken from an original copy, so neither printing nor grammatical errors have been corrected.

It is salutary to think back a mere sixty years – when sudden death was ever-present and a good night's sleep in your own bed a luxury; there was rationing, shortages, travel restrictions, censorship, and, always, fear for loved ones serving abroad or stationed somewhere in this country (often a guarded military secret).

Because so many of the men were away, the majority of casualties in Romford were women and children – so the fear for loved ones worked in both directions.

To bring back the memories of 'Business as usual', 'We never closed' and the sheer dogged courage of ordinary people is the intention of this re-issue.

The Borough of Romford in 1945

ORDEAL IN ROMFORD

BEING an account of Romford's sufferings
through enemy action 1940-1945—and a
tribute to the gallantry and fortitude of all
who were engaged in the task of combating
Nazi frightfulness, succouring the stricken,
maintaining community life in the face of
immense and unprecedented difficulties —
in other words, a recognition of
the contribution of the average
man and woman towards
the sum total of

VICTORY

PREFACE

" ORDEAL IN ROMFORD " is produced under the auspices of the Romford Mutual Help Association to serve two purposes. The first is to place on permanent record details of the trials which the Borough suffered as a front-line town during the war years. The second is to produce good from evil. The whole of the profits derived from the publication of this book will be devoted to local charities affiliated to the Mutual Help Association.

Those affiliated during the war were :—

VICTORIA HOSPITAL.
ROMFORD SOCIAL SERVICE ASSOCIATION.
ROMFORD TUBERCULOSIS CARE ASSOCIATION.
ROMFORD DISTRICT NURSING ASSOCIATION.
COLLIER ROW DISTRICT NURSING ASSOCIATION.
ROMFORD CIVIL DEFENCE BENEVOLENT FUND.
ROMFORD CIGARETTES FOR THE TROOPS FUND.
ROMFORD TROOPS WELFARE FUND.
RAINBOW CLUB FOR THE BLIND.
HAVERING DISTRICT NURSING ASSOCIATION.
ROMFORD GIRLS' AID COMMITTEE.

Just as Romford stood up to its ordeal as a result of the team-work of all sections of the community, this book is also the result of a combined effort to make it as complete and factual as possible. Sincere appreciation is expressed to the Romford Borough Council, without whose invaluable support and assistance the publication of this book would not have been possible, to Thompson's Photo Services, Ltd., Manor Park; Gordon Paule Press Photos, Romford; Messrs. Wilson & Whitworth Ltd., and The South Essex Recorders Ltd., for permission to use many of the pictures contained in this volume; to Mr. E. E. Willis (chairman) and Mr. John Grayston, G.M. (vice-chairman), of the Romford Mutual Help Association, for their co-operation, and to Mr. Stuart Titcombe for his artistic and symbolic drawing for the cover.

This book is commended to the people of Romford as a record of what they endured, and to posterity as an example of how the town faced the trials of a major war, which was fought in every street and in which ALL—men, women and children alike— were participants.

GLYN RICHARDS.

ROMFORD.

October, 1945.

NOTE.—Publication of this volume has been considerably delayed for reasons of security. The Editor is grateful to Mr. T. Macpherson, M.P., for his indefatigable efforts to obtain Departmental approval of its contents.

FOREWORD

BY

THE MAYOR OF ROMFORD
(ALDERMAN A. J. DYER, O.B.E., J.P.)

Looking back in retrospect on the last six years and remembering what Romford and those people who lived in it during that period have experienced, I find it in my heart to say how thankful I am that a divine providence does not permit us to anticipate the future. Had we known on September 3rd, 1939, after hearing the then Prime Minister's talk on the Wireless, and being told that we were in a state of war with Germany, and almost immediately hearing the first " alert " sounded, what we were to endure for the next 5½ years, I think that the strongest of us would have faced the future with considerable diffidence.

We are indeed fortunate that the loss of life, injury to our Townspeople, and material damage, have been comparatively small. But what has been the effect on our lives? My sympathy goes immediately to the children who have lost almost 6 years of their childhood, a loss which cannot be repaired. For nearly 6 years we have lived restricted lives—lives hemmed in with orders, regulations and rationing—but we know our neighbours far better than we did before. Our common danger tended to make us more friendly and sympathetic with those with whom we came into contact. Many friendships have been formed as a result of our experiences, and with many of us those friendships will not be lightly dropped.

I am glad beyond measure that it has been my honour and privilege to be the Chief Citizen of Romford when peace was declared, not only in Europe, but also in the Japanese theatre of war. We hoped that that honour would have fallen to my predecessor, but that was not to be.

In introducing this book to the people of Romford, I pay tribute on behalf of the Council to the members of the Civil Defence Organisation in the Borough, which carried out its difficult task with commendable courage, and by its efficiency saved many lives and prevented many more serious incidents. No individual or service can be singled out for commendation. All worked as part of the machinery of the service, and these remarks apply equally to the Police, the Wardens, the Shelter Controllers, the Fire Guards, the Fire Service, the Women's Voluntary Services, and the Public Utility Undertakings, as well as to the actual Civil Defence Services, which embraced the Rescue Service, the Road Repair Squads, the First-Aid Services, the Ambulance Service, the Messenger Service, and the Report and Control Service.

3

I would also like to compliment and pay tribute to my fellow townsfolk for the courage and endurance with which they faced their long ordeal; to the ordinary men and women who went quietly about their duties after many sleepless nights and nerve-racking experiences; to the tradespeople whose motto was always " Business as Usual "; and to the children who went to school " in between the warnings," and then, having got to school, spent half their school hours either in or running to and from the shelters.

This publication will have been justified if it serves but to commemorate the 143 civilians (the majority of them women and children) who lost their lives as a result of the enemy's indiscriminate attacks upon our home town.

ALBERT J. DYER.

October, 1945.

BOMBARDMENT OF ROMFORD

THE STORY

No apology is needed for presenting this story of Romford under enemy air attack, even though there were no spectacular raids, of the Baedeker variety, on the town as an individual target which served to bring it into the news, as was the case with some cities in other parts of the country. This is rather a story of a large number of relatively minor, but, nevertheless cumulatively serious, incidents spread over a period of years, which in sum total of casualties and damage were, in proportion, as serious as in almost any place in the country, outside London. It is probable that the strain on the townspeople was greater than in towns where a comparatively few heavy and concentrated attacks were made. Statistics are often misleading, but those given in later pages, coupled with the photographs, cannot fail to convey some indication of Romford's ordeal. Even on those dates where no " incident " is recorded, there is every probability that one of the 1,200 or so " Alerts " was sounded, and when this happened it was exceptional if enemy planes did not pass over the town to the usual accompaniment of a barrage from the neighbouring anti-aircraft guns.

It was often with a feeling of incredulity that we emerged from our air-raid shelters with the dawn, after a night with a continuous drone of enemy bombers passing overhead and the roar of guns mixed with all kinds of " other noises," to find that Romford was still there, and to learn in reply to the query " Anything in Romford last night? " that there had been no local incident. Apart from the actual bombs, it was not particularly pleasant to be abroad during a barrage, which would probably include the local " favourite " popularly known as " Whalebone Annie "—minor damage from shell splinters was frequent and on many occasions anti-aircraft shells failed to explode until they returned to earth. Two fatal casualties were caused in this way, apart from other " incidents " which caused appreciable damage.

It was no doubt due to its proximity to London, and to the fact that the outer ring of balloon and gun defences was just to the west that Romford received its undue proportion of attention from the enemy. Nazi 'planes, unable to penetrate these defences, would dispose of their bomb-load before turning back, but it was small comfort to Romfordians to know that they were not really the " target for to-night " and that the bombs they were receiving were intended for London proper.

Taken over the whole period of Bomb, Flying Bomb and Rocket attacks, only a few hundreds of the 18,000 houses in the Borough escaped damage, and some premises were damaged on as many as six occasions. No spot in the whole borough was more than a few yards away from some " incident " (ignoring incendiary bombs), and in one area of Collier Row five rockets and three flying bombs fell within a radius of 1,000 feet—surely something near a record.

The story, in chronological order, really commences as far back as 1935, when the Council, in common with all other local authorities, was asked to consider in very broad outline their plans for defence against air attack, with the saving clause that such measures " in no way imply a risk of war in the near future and they are wholly precautionary."

The initial " Alert " on the 3rd September, 1939 (which was actually a false alarm, as was that which sounded during the night of September 3rd-4th) was followed by an " Alert " about 7.30 a.m. on September 6th, during which an aeroplane passed over the town and a gun at the Whalebone battery fired three or four rounds. There was much excitement and speculation during the day, and the general opinion was that the aeroplane was, in fact, a British one. Nevertheless, Romford felt, somewhat proudly, that it had had its baptism of fire !

For the next few months, in keeping with the progress of the War in England, things were quiet, but the work of providing public shelters at various strategic points was completed so that by the time the Battle of France in 1940 was over there was accommodation for some 6,763 persons to be seated in these shelters. Subsequently, bunks were introduced to replace seats, and the accommodation accordingly reduced to provide sleeping space for 2,589 people. By August, 1940, it was clear that the enemy would launch large-scale air attacks against London at any moment, and everyone was busily putting the final touches to the " Anderson " shelters and incorporating various ideas and comforts. Many of us failed to appreciate that it would be necessary to spend more than an hour or two at a time in shelters, and, in due course, when we found that all-night sessions were to be expected as a regular thing, many pet gadgets had to give place to bunk-room, and much ingenuity had to be expended in converting a shelter which easily accommodated six persons sitting into a bedroom which, with great difficulty, housed the same number lying down.

THE FIRST BOMB

On August 28th, 1940, the first bomb fell in Romford ! We had been inclined to console ourselves with the fact that there was really nothing in Romford worth bombing, and the optimists felt that the most we need worry about was a stray bomb or two. We did not realise at the time, perhaps, how indiscriminate and inaccurate the bombing would be, nor that it was the enemy's object to terrorise the civil population rather than to concentrate on legitimate objectives. Anyway, *our* bomb had arrived, and

This bomb crater was caused in the garden of "Strathmore," Main Road, Romford, which was being used at the time as a boarding house.

The upheaval of a gas main in Dagenham Road, near the Romford Cemetery, by a bomb, which made a deep crater.

Smashed premises in Victoria Road, as seen on September 14th, 1940.

we could now hold up our heads with neighbouring Hornchurch, whose bomb had fallen some days before! A large part of the population visited Jubilee Avenue, the scene of the incident, and although, in the light of later experience, the small crater in the road with the damaged windows and roofs of adjacent houses was not really spectacular, most of the sightseers were satisfied with the evidence that Romford was in the front line. Those who had been " unfortunate " enough not to hear the bomb whistle down were very anxious to know what it sounded like, and wondered if they would ever get the chance to hear another. There was no need for such anxiety, for even the most sensationally-minded were soon to hear them often enough to become connoisseurs, and to be able to pick out the sound instantaneously from the bedlam of other noises.

THE BATTLE OF BRITAIN

With the Battle of Britain at the end of August and during September, the sirens commenced to wail in real earnest, and it became commonplace to make a dash for the shelter with a half-eaten meal in one hand and a cup of tea in the other. From the shelter entrance, in those sunny summer days, we had many a grandstand view of the might of the Luftwaffe coming up high over the Thames, dozens of little silvery specks flying in formation against the blue sky, only to see them scatter as the white puffs of anti-aircraft shells burst among them. And then we would hear the drone of our fighters as the guns eased off, and the sky would be criss-crossed by the vapour trails of the aircraft as they manoeuvred and fought above. From the ground below, some of these combats were so remote as often to be out of sight and sound, and it was not until we heard on the wireless the latest " score " of enemy aeroplanes destroyed that we reaslised how our fate was being settled over our heads.

Saturday, August 31st, was one of the more exciting of such days. The " Alert " sounded for the third time that day at 1.10 p.m., and not long afterwards a German aeroplane, flying low, passed over the town with a British fighter chasing it close behind with machine guns blazing. As it passed over the Victoria Road area, a stick of bombs was released, obviously jettisoned to facilitate the escape. The bombs demolished houses and killed several people. The German aircraft was destroyed by the pursuing Spitfire. This was one of the few occasions on which bombs from piloted aircraft fell in daylight. Just before 6 p.m. another " Alert " sounded, and on this occasion an enemy aeroplane crashed to earth on the Whalebone gun site and burst into flames. Portions of the machine dropped in various parts of the town and the pilot was seen parachuting down from a tremendous height. At first it seemed to each one of us that he would be dropping in our own back garden, and in some cases

7

a " reception committee " was hurriedly formed in anticipation (as was actually the case) that he would prove to be a German. However, as he descended lower, he was caught by the ground currents, and drifted away in the direction of Hornchurch, where he was finally captured on the land occupied by the Council's Sewage Works.

By this time, raids during the night were also becoming a regular thing, and it became the usual procedure to take bedding into the shelters. It was interesting to note how quickly we adapted ourselves to the new routine, although even then we did not foresee the dreary succession of nights to come, which grew worse as the days shortened, and which we were to be condemned to spend underground. The number of incidents in Romford also began to increase, and we began to get accustomed to the terrific barrage which seemed to be sounding all night and every night. That some of the raiders were successful in reaching London became apparent from the huge ring of fires which could frequently be seen on the skyline. Incendiary bombs were also dropping in the Romford area, though little damage was done on the first few occasions.

THE FIRST MINE

Throughout September, the enemy continued night after night, commencing with almost clockwork regularity with the onset of darkness, to press home his attack on London, and began using heavier bombs and something that was new to us— the parachute mine, or " land-mine " as it was popularly, but wrongly, known. One of these fell during the night of September 21st-22nd between Stanley Avenue and Carlton Road. Casualties were fortunately light, but fantastic tales were told of the size of the crater, and we felt we must revise some of our ideas of possible bomb damage. This new weapon was certainly devastating, as we were to learn later on, and from a psychological point of view was, to many people, more terrifying than even the Flying Bomb or the Rocket of later times. Certainly the damage caused was generally at least equal to, if not greater than, that caused by the latter weapons. The explosion of this first mine broke a number of shop windows in South Street.

On September 23rd, one of the Germans' parachute mines dropped on a vacant piece of land in Birkbeck Road at approximately 11.30 at night, and it remained a source of interest to Romford people for two days. Fortunately it did not explode, but its constant threat to do so resulted in the temporary evacuation of about 1,000 people from the Birkbeck Estate. This was the largest evacuation we had to face during the war and our resources were taxed to the utmost extent. The Mawney Road Rest Centre was opened, the Carlisle Institute was taken over in the middle of the night by arrangement with the Con-

The rear of houses in Stanley Avenue, Gidea Park, following the bursting of Romford's first mine on the night of September 21st/22nd, 1940.

Seventeen houses were demolished in Stanley Avenue and Carlton Road, and many hundreds were damaged. This picture shows furniture being moved out of some of the affected property on the following day.

The gutted furniture store of Messrs. Henry Haysom, in North Street, photographed the day after the severe raid on October 13th, 1940.

These ancient wooden houses in North Street caught fire when a bomb hit Messrs. Haysom's store, opposite, on October 13th, 1940.

gregational Church authorities, and the remainder of the evacuated people who could not be accommodated in these buildings were sent to the shelters in Cottons Recreation Ground and to other public shelters, some as far away as those in front of the Town Hall and next to the Baptist Church in Main Road. By quick and efficient improvisation it was practicable to provide the enforced evacuees with some refreshments and blankets during the night and, though many of them doubtless spent several uncomfortable nights away from their homes they were fortunate in being able, in due course, to return to their undamaged houses. The mine was rendered harmless by the Bomb Disposal Squad on September 25th, and on October 5th was removed from Birkbeck Road to Bedfords Park, where it was successfully disposed of by the Borough Surveyor (Mr. F. V. Appleby) and the Rescue Squad and, greatly to their relief, the evacuated families were able to return to their homes.

OIL BOMBS

On the night of October 13th a number of oil incendiary bombs dropped in the town. One at Oldchurch Hospital and one in the Brewery Yard were extinguished before doing much damage. A further oil bomb which fell in the ale house at the Brewery fortunately failed to ignite. But more serious fires were caused near the North Street/Church Lane junction, where Messrs. Haysom's commodious furniture store was completely gutted and other neighbouring properties damaged, and also at the Romford Telephone Exchange. A message was received in the Report Centre at 9.26 p.m., that the Exchange was being evacuated and that no further messages in or out could be taken. The fire was eventually subdued, and by 10.5 p.m. the telephones were again working.. In the meantime the Messenger Service had to operate as incidents had occurred as a result of bombs dropped in Netherpark Drive and at Collier Row.

WIDESPREAD BOMBING

October 16th brought a night which will be remembered by all the members of the Civil Defence Services who had to be abroad. The weather was appalling, and it was fondly hoped for once there would be a break in the long succession of sirens, and that the rain would keep the Luftwaffe grounded. We did not then appreciate that weather had little effect upon bombing missions. Soon after 7 p.m. the Alert sounded, to continue in operation for the next eleven hours. Within half an hour the first bomb had fallen in the roadway in Pettits Lane, igniting a gas main, and five minutes later two parachute mines fell at Havering, damaging a large number of the houses in the village. Half an hour later a stick of bombs fell across Lawns Recreation

9

Ground and nearby roads, a shelter being hit in the garden of a house in The Drive and five persons killed. Rescue work was made extremely difficult by climatic conditions, and the craters were in some cases nearly filled with water. Further bombs at Pyrgo Park and to the north-east of Rise Park fortunately fell in the open, but half-an-hour before midnight a further stick of bombs screamed down in the area of Cottons Recreation Ground. London Road was blocked by a delayed action bomb which fell in the roadway near Messrs. C. H. Allen's Garage (this exploded some five hours later), houses were damaged in Richards Avenue and Recreation Avenue, and a Public Shelter in Cottons was hit, causing six more fatal casualties; other shelterers had remarkable escapes from death. This was the only occasion on which people were killed in a public shelter, although on several occasions occupants were shaken by near " misses."

LULL AFTER 61 NIGHTS

November 3rd was an outsanding night, but for a different reason—it was the first night since September 1st on which no warning sounded, and broke a succession of 61 nights. To many people this " break " was unexpected, and rather than being caught indoors, they spent the night underground as a matter of routine. The lull was only temporary, for the following evening it was " siren as usual."

Many of us, after weeks on end of cramped accommodation in our shelters, were beginning to spend the nights in the house, and it was not always merely a question of comfort but of necessity, for many shelters had become waterlogged with the onset of wet weather. But whatever the reason, whether voluntary or by force of circumstances, there is no doubt that the tendency to sleep indoors increased the number of casualties, although some of the fortunate ones did actually save their lives by changing their routine. The figures show, however, that for each house demolished in September or October, there was roughly one casualty, but that during November and December the figure rose to over three casualties per house demolished.

During November there was an easing off in the number of incidents, many of the bombs falling in the more open parts of the Borough, although a number of casualties and widespread damage was caused by a heavy bomb of unusual type which fell in Cedric Avenue on November 24th. The proportion of bombs which failed to explode on impact (being either of the delayed action type or faulty ones) increased. The centre of the town had a particularly lucky escape when a whole stick of bombs, which dropped across it on November 4th, failed to explode. South Street was closed to traffic until one of these, in the roadway outside the Havana Cinema, had been removed by the Bomb Disposal Squad.

10

The huge crater caused by the Carlton Road-Stanley Avenue parachute mine on the night of September 21/22nd, 1940.

White Hart Lane, Collier Row, after the attack on October 2nd, 1940.

The wrecked Romford Telephone Exchange at the rear of South Street, which suffered vom a parachute mine on December 8th, 1940.

A NIGHT OF TERROR

The shopping centre of Romford was remarkably fortunate throughout the war years in not suffering any devastating incident, though South Street presented a sorry sight on the morning of December 9th, 1940, with the roadway strewn with debris and glass, mixed with goods from shop windows. In a few hours things looked almost normal with the shop fronts temporarily repaired, except in the immediate vicinity of Exchange Street, where a parachute mine had fallen during the night, completely demolishing a blacksmith's shop, partly demolishing the Telephone Exchange and seriously damaging nearby shops and a portion of the Brewery. One of the " lighter " episodes of the incident was the story of the anvil, weighing a quarter of a ton, from the blacksmith's shop, which was blown into the air right over the White Hart Hotel and finally crashed to earth through the roof of a shelter at the rear of a butcher's shop on the other side of High Street, falling between two of the occupants in the shelter and only slightly grazing one of them ! The anvil was subsequently put on show by the enterprising tradesman and raised an appreciable sum for local charities ! But on the other side of the picture, this was one of the most difficult nights which the Civil Defence Services were to experience. There were an unusual number of incidents and almost the first was a parachute mine on the A.R.P. Depot in Oldchurch Road, where most of the ambulances and other vehicles and much valuable stores and records were destroyed. This meant that practically half of the Council's available appliances were out of action immediately and that the remaining Depot at Havering Road would have to cover all incidents. Meanwhile, bombs were also dropping in various parts of the Borough, and before the Report Centre could get any picture of what had happened, the telephones went " dead " as another parachute mine put the Telephone Exchange out of action for the rest of the night (and for some weeks so far as ordinary subscribers were concerned). From that time onwards, communications had to be maintained by means of messengers (many of them lads in their 'teens) and no praise is too high for the splendid work which they and the whole of the Services did on this difficult occasion. At the best of times, it was not easy to maintain control when incidents were numerous, and with half the appliances out of action and no telephone communication possible, the difficulties were increased a hundredfold. Contact was eventually established with County Control Centre at Chelmsford via the Plough Corner Police Station, and mutual assistance in the way of vehicles, etc., was made available from Brentwood and Hornchurch. In the meantime, other bombs and mines were dropping in such widely separated parts of the Borough as Rush Green, London Road, Colchester Road, Carlton Road, Collier Row and Havering. Three bombs fell on the

11

Romford Gas Works, but, by a miracle, there were no personal injuries. One bomb made a direct hit on the purifiers, another was a near miss on one of the gas holders, and the third hit a gas holder and set it on fire. For their courage on this memorable night, Mr. John Grayston, Engineer of the Company, and Mr. Bert Poole, shift foreman, were each awarded the George Medal. It was with a sigh of relief that the Report Centre staff finally cleared at 6.15 a.m. the last of the thirty or so incidents which had given them one of their most difficult nights.

Further parachute mines fell in Balgores Lane on the night of December 27th, and although one did a considerable amount of damage, the other failed to explode. This latter was removed to Portsmouth by the Naval authorities at 2.30 p.m. on the following day, and Balgores Lane and the neighbouring roads were re-opened to traffic, and the public, who had been evacuated, allowed to return home.

500 INCENDIARIES

The year 1941 opened quietly, with a marked reduction in the number of incidents. It was not until March 9th that the first really serious incident of the year occurred, when a heavy bomb fell in the centre of Wolseley Road causing a very large crater and a number of casualties and considerable damage. The lull was further shattered by upwards of 500 explosive incendiary bombs which were scattered over a wide area on the night of March 15th. The worst concentrations were in the area of Main Road, Gidea Park, and Victoria Road, but thanks to the exertions of firewatchers and the public generally (who were quick to smother the bombs with sandbags, despite the risk of an explosion at any second), and to good work by the N.F.S. no serious fires developed, though the roofs and upper storeys of a number of properties suffered damage. There was a number of casualties and while these were under treatment at Oldchurch Hospital, three bombs completely demolished the Medical Superintendent's block, which was, fortunately, empty at the time.

ROMFORD'S WORST NIGHT

The next outstanding night was that of April 19/20th, which was, without doubt, the worst from the point of view of damage and casualties which Romford sustained throughout the whole of the War years. It will always be remembered locally as the " Essex Road Night," and certainly this incident, though only one of many during the night, created an impression of horror in the minds of the townspeople which was never surpassed. Altogether eight parachute mines, three high explosive bombs, and a number of incendiaries dropped in Romford on that night, apart from a further mine which, although dropping

Hillfoot Avenue after the disastrous raid on April 25th, 1941.

The death roll in Essex Road on April 25th, 1941, was the heaviest of the war in Romford. This picture gives an idea of the devastation.

Many houses were destroyed in Brentwood Road in the great raid on April 25th, 1941.

What a bomb did in McIntosh Road-Cedric Avenue, Marshall's Park, on September 10/11th, 1940.

on the Hornchurch side of the boundary in Brentwood Road, demolished and damaged a large number of houses on the Romford side. One of the first mines fell on a terrace of houses in Essex Road and reduced many houses to piles of rubble. It was soon apparent that many casualties were buried under the debris and an appeal was made to County Control for mutual assistance, as a result of which First-aid Parties and Ambulances and Rescue Squads were despatched from Hornchurch. Further serious mine incidents were soon reported from Hillfoot Avenue, Carlisle Road/Princes Road and Pettits Lane, and further mutual aid was despatched from Brentwood. It speaks highly of the efficiency of these mutual aid arrangements that there was a lapse of only thirteen minutes on both occasions between the despatch of the message from the Romford Report Centre and the receipt of a message from County Control that the assistance was on the way. For the next four hours, while rescue parties were toiling at these four major incidents, the guns continued to thunder, and further mines fell at intervals, fortunately in more or less open country, though several of them were within a few hundred yards of Essex Road. Finally, the long-awaited "Raiders Passed" sounded, but there was no pause in the rescue work which continued throughout the following day. Additional Rescue Parties arrived from Chelmsford to take over from the still-willing but dead-tired parties which had toiled all night, and for the next two days supplementary casualty lists were published at intervals as further bodies were recovered. When it was possible to pause to take stock of the situation, it was found that, in all, there had been 127 casualties; 44 of them fatal, and that 93 houses had been demolished and upwards of 2,000 houses damaged. In other words, between 20 per cent. and 25 per cent. of the total casualties and damage sustained in the town during the whole War period occurred on this one night. The mass funeral service for many of the 38 Essex Road victims took place during the following week at St. John's Church and was attended by a large number of local residents as well as by representatives of the Borough Council and of the Civil Defence Services.

Just as in battlefield operations there are sometimes some seemingly inexplicable survivals, there was one such in Essex Road which caused all who saw it to reflect upon its significance. At a spot where many houses were mere heaps of rubble a small triangular piece of wall stood with a short length of picture rail still adhering to it. Hanging from this picture rail was a framed copy of Holman Hunt's famous picture, "The Light of the World," intact in every way, and its glass unimpaired. In a sea of devastation the "Light of the World" remained—a reminder and a challenge!

The night of May 10th/11th brought further parachute mines in the Gidea Park area, and though damage to property was widespread, casualties were, fortunately, light. One mine completely demolished All Saint's Church, Squirrels Heath, and the other fell in Castellan Avenue, the latter causing the death of one man.

MACHINE GUNNING RAID

Raids were by now very sporadic, and apart from July 28th, 1941, when four bombs within a small radius caused casualties and damage at the junction of Catherine Road and Hamilton Road, the only incidents for nearly the next two years were from anti-aircraft shells or by the belated discovery of a number of unexploded bombs which had fallen in outlying districts during the 1940 blitz period.

In the morning of March 12th, 1943, a number of fast enemy planes which had flown up the Thames estuary, probably on reconnaissance, turned inland and returned to the coast via Ilford and Romford. Just after 7.30 a.m. the planes swept over Romford at roof-top height with machine guns blazing, following roughly the line of the railway. For a short time bedlam was let loose, and people on their way to work had lucky escapes, including many waiting on Romford station, who had a grandstand view. The only serious damage was at the Gas Works where three of the gasholders were set ablaze, and in Balmoral Road where a water main was fractured. The gasholder fire was extinguished by 11.30 a.m.

FIRE RAISING

Only a few bombs fell in the remainder of 1943, and these were mostly in outlying districts. Scattered raids by a comparatively small number of fast bombers continued into 1944, and during an incendiary raid in the early morning of January 22nd, 1944, many houses were ablaze in the Albert Road and Victoria Road area, and a serious fire occurred at the Bottling Department and in the Hop Store of the Brewery, which blazed fiercely for some hours before it was brought under control. A total of 27 fire pumps were in action at this fire. A German aeroplane was brought down by anti-aircraft fire on February 3rd, and crashed in a field between Lower Bedfords Road and Havering Road North. One of the crew who managed to bale out was taken in an injured condition to Oldchurch Hospital, but the other two members crashed with the 'plane, which burst into flames, and for some time was visible like a beacon from all over Romford. The bodies of the two airmen were interred, with representatives of our own Royal Air Force present as bearers, in Romford Cemetery a few days later.

April 19th brought another incendiary bomb raid which was mainly concentrated in the High Street and South Street areas. Serious fires quickly developed at the Brewery, at Messrs. Allen's

14

Castellan Avenue, Gidea Park, suffered from the explosion of a parachute mine, which did widespread damage on May 10th, 1941.

The ruins of All Saints' Church, Squirrels Heath, as seen on the morning of May 11th, 1941. The Cross-shaped window shows intact against the sky, while the little wooden steeple can be seen on a heap of rubble in the foreground.

Messrs. C. H. Allen's garage, and adjoining property, in London Road ablaze during the height of the fire blitz on Romford, an April 19th, 1944.

Garage in London Road, at the Salvation Army Citadel, and in a number of shops and private houses in the surrounding area, though a very large number of the bombs, particularly those which fell in the roadway in South Street and High Street, were extinguished quickly by the Fireguards. As soon as the " Raiders Passed " sounded, crowds of townspeople made their way to the scene of the fires, which were the most spectacular seen in Romford during the war period, the whole of the centre of the town being lit up for hours in startling contrast to the black-out which had been the rule for so long. By the next morning, all the fires had been extinguished or had burned themselves out. Fire Service personnel attended from as far away as Ipswich to deal with the conflagration. Among the premises destroyed were Messrs. Allen's garage, the bottling store at the Brewery, and the Salvation Army junior hall as well as a number of houses in streets leading off London Road. A woman lost her life through being struck by an incendiary bomb when going to her shelter.

FLY BOMBS

This was the last of the incidents as we had for so long known them and raids from piloted aircraft were soon to be a thing of the past, but this did not mean that our ordeal was yet over. In June, confidential information was received that a new form of attack might be expected, and Civil Defence quietly prepared to meet the new menace under its code name of " Flys." The man in the street was also speculating upon the news that a German " aeroplane " had crashed near Coborn Road L.N.E.R. Station, the pilot of the machine being mysteriously absent. Unknown to most of the population, however, the sirens which sounded on the night of June 15th, 1944, heralded a new era of enemy atrocity, and was the beginning of the nightmare weeks of flying bombs with their harsh rattling roar, followed by the awful period of suspense after the engine " cut out." At these moments we were soon to learn that time literally stood still, and that when the explosion did come it was almost a relief, even if one's roof and windows were blown in. The siren had not sounded long on this memorable night before the anti-aircraft batteries were in full blast against mysterious aircraft which were flying fast and low and which appeared to be crashing and exploding with all their bombs on board at a rate which soon exceeded the most optimistic score of any previous raid. By the time the sixth or seventh had been " shot down," the layman began to revise his ideas and to come to realise that he was experiencing some-thing new. Slowly the night wore on and still the nightmare of sounds continued, until, with the coming of daylight, there was a lull, although the final comfort of the " Raiders Passed " was still denied us until well into the morning. Many probably shared the impression of a firewatcher on that first night, who, towards

15

the dawn, fell into an uneasy doze of a few minutes on the step of his " post," and who said afterwards that, when he was awakened by a louder crash than usual, and saw the sky full of tracers and flaming onions with mysterious lights speeding along only to disappear with a blinding flash and a terrific roar, he thought for a few moments he was dead and in hell (where, perhaps, he deserved to be in any event for sleeping at his post !). An announcement on the wireless the next day gave official information on the new form of attack, and it relieved the tension to know more exactly what we were facing, even if it did confirm our worst suspicions.

Incidentally, it is interesting to speculate how far, from a psychological angle, the adoption by the public of the unofficial name of " Doodlebug " assisted in maintaining morale. After we had started calling it by odd and uncomplimentary names and had heard a few clever (but unprintable) stories about it, the flying bomb did not seem quite so fearsome, and it may well be that some unknown and unrecognised humorist did greater work than he imagined when he gave the appellation " Doodlebug " to these uncanny missiles, and possibly almost ranks for inclusion among the " back room boys "!

In the Report Centre, a message had been received from County Control that " Flys " had commenced falling at 11.50 p.m., and within a short time, local confirmation of this was forthcoming (if any were needed!) by reports of " Flys " falling in Romford —at Collier Row and in Barton Avenue. The latter incident gave the services some indication of what to expect, with damage and casualties comparable with the parachute mine of earlier days, and it was comforting to see that the Civil Defence personnel had not gone " rusty " during their months of comparative inactivity, but that, on the contrary, they were on the job as speedily and as efficiently as ever.

Space will not permit a description of all the incidents from Flying Bombs which fell in the Borough—to say nothing of, literally, the hundreds which roared over, or which, after " cutting-out " overhead, glided over the boundary instead of diving on our heads in the more orthodox fashion—but mention must be made of some of the more serious ones. In the early light of June 17th a Flying Bomb which fell in the roadway in Lodge Lane, a few yards beyond Collier Row Road, caused a number of casualties and demolished houses on both sides of the road. Four mornings later, on June 21st, at roughly the same time, another fell at the rear of Hainault Road and Collier Row Lane, the casualties and damage in this more populous area being considerable. After three less serious incidents, more casualties and damage occurred in the evening of the 25th, when a Flying Bomb fell in Clockhouse Lane nearly opposite the School.

The problem of repairs to damaged houses was by now becoming a serious one, as incidents followed at more or less

How an anti-personnel bomb left one of the stands at the Romford Stadium on October 9th, 1940.
The bomb pitched on the judges' box in the centre of the arena, and made it disappear—not so
much as a bolt being found afterwards. Widespread damage was done to the track and buildings.
Two clubs were badly smashed. The Stadium suffered three times in the course of the war.

Another stand on the opposite side of the Stadium, which was smashed on October 9th, 1940.

Shops in the rear of South Street, battered by the mine on December 8th, 1940.

Members of the A.F.S. got their "baptism of fire" when dealing with this blaze in Victoria Road, caused by incendiary bombs.

regular intervals—each incident involved repairs to windows, roofs, etc., of some hundreds of houses, and workmen were sent to the district from " quieter " parts of the country to give much needed assistance. The next incident was in the evening of June 30th, when houses and shops on both sides of the L.N.E.R. line were blasted by a bomb which was hit by gunfire, and crashed on the line just east of Romford Station. Casualties on this occasion were remarkably light, though only a few yards away large numbers of people were in South Street and the cinemas, etc. Officially, there was no " Alert " at the time, and there was some local comment on this and on the suggestion that but for having been crippled by gunfire the bomb would possibly have passed over Romford into the open country to the north. Shortly after this, the practice of firing at the robots while over built-up areas was discontinued, and, without knowing it at the time, we heard the local guns for the last time on July 15th.

A further serious incident occurred during the night of July 7th/8th in Mawney Road, near its junction with Percy Road. As on previous occasions, the casualties were quickly dealt with, and many lives were undoubtedly saved during the Flying Bomb phase by the speed with which the various services arrived on the spot— usually only a matter of a very few minutes after the occurrence. Flying squads were always standing by, and, where possible, even followed in the flight of the bomb so as to be on the spot as quickly as possible after it fell.

THE GREAT EXODUS

Incidents in the Borough had by now been sufficiently numerous and serious to warrant the extension of the Government's Evacuation Scheme to the area, and on July 14th, when the main parties left, and on subsequent dates, a total of some 9,847 mothers and children left the " front line " for quieter parts of the country. Most of the unaccompanied children went to North Suffolk and South Norfolk, where the residents of Beccles, Bungay, and other towns and villages looked after their safety and comfort in a most charming and courteous manner, and were really sorry to lose them when they officially returned home in June, 1945. Other evacuees went to Barnsley, Blaby (near Leicester), Derby, Middlesbrough and Sheffield.

There were only two more serious Flying Bomb incidents, to follow, one between Gorseway and Rush Green Road in the morning of August 5th, and one at the junction of Hillfoot Road and Collier Row Lane during the night of August 6th/7th. This latter Flying Bomb made a silent approach, having given its final vicious " cough " somewhere over the Thames, but the searchlights which continued to sweep along with the bomb during the remainder of its flight gave warning of its approach to those who were still abroad as it speeded silently over the Market Place and on to Collier Row.

17

With the capture of the launching sites in France the worst appeared to be over, though after a lapse we once again heard the old familiar roar, this time coming from east to west instead of the previous south to north direction. These flying bombs, we are told, were launched from enemy 'planes near the coast, and though a fair number passed over Romford (some of them dangerously near the roof tops), the attacks were intermittent, and only one fell within the boundary, namely, at Noak Hill, on October 5th.

HITLER'S LAST WEAPON

Up to this time there had been remarkably few occasions on which the sirens had failed to give warning of the imminence of enemy attack, but during the next few months all this was changed, for already, before the last Flying Bomb had fallen, mysterious " somethings " were beginning to fall with a mighty explosion, followed by a long thundering rumble and then another " crack," and, moreover, without the slightest warning. We heard of an " explosion " at Chiswick and of some " defective gas mains " in a school at Dagenham, and later we heard officially of the V.2's. The Civil Defence Services were warned in advance of the possibility of a new bomb and kept the news to themselves. It was not until the information was officially released that the outside public knew anything of it.

These new weapons, originally known by the code name of " Big Ben," were later officially recorded in the Report Centre incident log as " Wasps." The explosions of these " rockets " could be heard for many miles. Altogether 21 fell within the Borough boundary, but many more (including those just beyond the boundary) were close enough to give that momentary mental shock which, after some months, began to try even the strongest nerves. However, everyone had to carry on as usual and hope for the best, from the children going to school (though some of the younger ones were encouraged to put their heads under the desk if the first " bang " was very loud) to the old age pensioners doing their shopping and holding their weekly meetings. It is indeed a matter for congratulation that the bulk of these projectiles fell in more or less open country, as it is also terrifying to visualise the results if one had fallen in, say, the Market Place or in South Street on a busy day.

Within a short time of the introduction of the Rocket, one fell at Noak Hill, on September 16th, 1944, and various parts which were recovered were of considerable interest to the experts. Meanwhile, the man in the street was feeling a trifle puzzled that no mention of these " incidents " was being made officially, and he felt a little hurt that once again London and district was " taking it " apparently quite unknown to official circles and to the rest of the country. It was realised, however, that this was

18

Another view of the devastation at the Romford Brewery on April 19th, 1944.

A revealing picture of the effect of a rocket in Collier Row Lane on November 15th, 1944.

only part of a policy to keep the enemy guessing as to the success and range of his new weapon, and from then on, the public entered into the spirit of the Government's decision and voluntarily assisted in maintaining secrecy by refusing to talk much of their experiences, especially to strangers. It is in keeping with a Briton's character that much more would probably have been said had there been some official request for secrecy !

At length the ban was lifted, and the public learned officially that the enemy was launching long-range rockets against what was described as " Southern England," and that after their journey through the stratosphere, reaching a height of some 60 miles, they travelled to earth at a speed exceeding that of sound. It was rather disconcerting to see for the first time a diagram of one of these monsters, even if the warhead, with its ton or so of high explosive, did appear only as an insignificant section in the nose. It was difficult not to dwell on the possibility of one being even at that moment speeding on its way down towards us, like a giant dart with ourselves as the " bull." A few people, who had happened to be looking in the right spot at the right moment, had seen the burst of smoke from the overhead explosion and a shining streak shoot to earth, but most of us realised that we should be very lucky indeed if we ever knew what had hit us.

After several further Rockets had fallen, more or less in the open, the first serious incident occurred, in Ainsley Avenue, on November 15th, 1944, to be followed the next morning by another shattering explosion near the junction of Rosedale Road and Collier Row Lane, which shook the whole of Romford. This neighbourhood had already suffered considerably from a nearby Flying Bomb, and the second wave of devastation was widespread and resulted in the most serious Rocket incident in Romford, and, in fact, one of the most serious in the whole of Essex. While photographs can give some idea of the terrible damage caused, they cannot portray the real horror of the scene as the rescue parties got to work almost before the dust had settled, nor of the widespread damage caused for hundreds of yards around. Of the 83 casualties, 13 were fatal and 32 persons had to be admitted to hospital. Apart from the 34 houses which were demolished, over 800 others were damaged. Rescue work continued for many hours, and trained Alsatian dogs assisted in locating some of the victims.

For the next three months, Rockets continued to fall, but by the beginning of 1945 the explosions were becoming more frequent, and we wondered how long our luck would last. It broke on February 20th, 1945, when a Rocket fell in Fairholme Avenue. The scene of destruction was illuminated by a mobile searchlight while the rescue work continued throughout the night, and Alsatian dogs again assisted. As a result of their efforts, further casualties were located, the total mounting to 62, including 12 persons killed.

LAST ROCKET—LAST SIREN

Less serious incidents during the succeeding month were followed by the final incidents of the War on March 26th, 1945. After an unusual triple explosion, a mushroom of smoke and dust could be seen, and we knew that Collier Row had " got it again "—this time in the roadway in Mawney Road near its junction with Forest Road; by a happy chance, the road at the time was more or less deserted, and though there was much damage and a number of casualties, only two proved fatal. The final incident at Noak Hill later the same evening caused little personal injury, but it wrecked the Village War Memorial Hall, and thus the end of the chapter was reached, for no further Rockets were to fall on England after the following morning. The next few days were also to bring the last occasion on which we should hear the sirens wail during the War—this was on March 29th, when the " Alert " sounded at 9.59 a.m., and the " All Clear " at 10.12 a.m., and that famliar sound which had for so many years formed the background of our waking and sleeping world was silent from now on. If the 1,264 " Alerts " had sounded one after the other, the wail would have continued for nearly two complete days and nights, with a more or less corresponding period for the " Raiders Passed."

Credit is due to every man, woman and child in every part of the Borough for the courage and fortitude which they showed during the trying years, of which only a glimpse has been given in the preceding pages. But it is felt that no one will begrudge a special salute to Collier Row for the courage with which it endured its undue share of prominence. Though it includes not much more than one quarter of the Borough, it suffered half the total of the fatal casualties and seemed to attract bombs, flying bombs and rockets with equal impartiality.

WERE THEY "INCIDENTS"?

The reader may have wondered long before this why all the major and serious occurrences which have been described are called " incidents," when this has been so often a completely inadequate term for them. For want of a better description, they have been so called officially since the commencement of Civil Defence, whether the occurrence were a shell nose-cap reported from the wide open spaces or a parachute mine in South Street. If your own particular " incident " has not already been mentioned, reference to it should at least be found in the " Diary " which follows, and which, perhaps, in its bare record of facts will serve to demonstrate better than any elaborate description the real extent of Romford's long ordeal.

20

Part of the immense damage done in Mawneys Road by a rocket on March 26th, 1945.

A flying bomb, which did not explode, on view in Romford Market Place in the cause of charity on October 18th, 1944.

Courage on a gas-holder at the Romford Gas Works on March 12th, 1943. The man in the asbestos suit is extinguishing fires caused by machine-gun bullets.

Two last notes should be made to complete this brief history of Romford's war-time experiences. The first is that Romford received almost the last German rocket which fell in this country. This was that which fell on March 26th, 1945, and to which reference has already been made. In fact, the last rocket to fall in this country fell early on the following morning.

The second is that, curious as it may seem, during the whole of the war period anyone visiting the Romford Market Place or South Street would never have visualised what Romford was suffering. Shops were opened as usual even though the bulk of them were boarded up, housewives were busy shopping, men were carrying on with their usual daily work, and children were going to school, and some of them were even tackling serious examination papers in air-raid shelters. The life of the town continued despite the attacks of the enemy, and despite the fact, as this history shows, that Romford was in the fighting line. The Local Government of the Borough continued without respite. Mayors were elected, Aldermen and Councillors were appointed, and the normal routine was followed in the most abnormal circumstances. Some of the Mayors during the war period had some arduous tasks to face. It was the custom of every Mayor to visit the scenes of incidents as quickly as possible after the incidents had occurred. They visited the sufferers in their homes and in hospital; they conveyed the sympathy of the Council to those who were the latest victims of Nazi bombing. The Mayor in 1941 attended at St. John's Church on April 29th, 1941, a mass funeral of 12 victims. The Mayor, in August, 1940, was on the scene of the first incident which occurred in the Borough. The Mayors in 1944 and 1945 had the unfortunate task of visiting those who had met with loss and damage by the German Fly Bombs and Rockets, and they further had to see off from and had the pleasure of welcoming back to the Town the mothers and children who were evacuated during the intensive bombing. From August, 1940, to May, 1945, the Mayor for the time being, with the assistance of a small Committee, was responsible for the administration of Romford's part of the Lord Mayor of London's Air-Raid Distress Fund. The " war period " Mayors of Romford did their duty loyally and well, and not only did they themselves live up to the Council's motto " Serve with Gladness," but they encouraged their fellow-townspeople to do likewise. It is a happy thought that the Coat of Arms bears its motto in English, and not in Latin which is only understood (or perhaps misunderstood) by lawyers and schoolmasters, and it is a humble suggestion to the future generations of Romfordians, who may happen to peruse this book, that they endeavour to emulate the Romfordians of the war period and serve their town with the same measure of willingness and gladness as was shown by its inhabitants during the World War from September, 1939, to May, 1945.

ROMFORD INCIDENTS

DAY BY DAY

AUGUST, 1940

27th ... 11.8 p.m.—H.E., Jubilee Avenue.
31st ... 1.20 p.m.—H.E.'s, Richmond Road, Randall Road (house demolished); King Edward Road, etc. (3 fatal casualties).

SEPTEMBER, 1940

5th ... 11.50 p.m.—H.E.'s, Lawnsway (house demolished) and near Clockhouse Lane/Lynwood Drive.
7th ... 6.0 p.m.—H.E.'s and Oil Bombs, Colchester Road, rear of Waverley Crescent and Noak Hill.
10th ... 2.11 a.m.—H.E., North Street/Eastern Avenue.
3.40 a.m.—H.E., St. John's Road (2 houses demolished).
4.23 a.m.—H.E., Pinewood Road.
10th/11th 10.4 p.m.—H.E.'s, Hill Grove (4 houses demolished), Pettits Lane, Dorset Avenue, Main Road, McIntosh Road/Cedric Avenue (2 houses demolished).
11.5 p.m.—H.E.'s, Highfield Road and Burland Road.
11.10 p.m.—H.E.'s, North of Colchester Road and on Maylands.
11.15 p.m.—H.E.'s, St. John's Road and Pinewood Road; H.E.'s, Bower Farm, Havering; Oil Bomb and H.E.'s Noak Hill.
11.27 p.m.—H.E., Erith Crescent.
11.30 p.m.—H.E., Chase Cross Road (house demolished).
12th/13th 10.45 p.m.—H.E., Shaftesbury Road.
10.50 p.m.—H.E.'s near Straight Road.
11.57 p.m.—H.E.'s, Victoria Road (3 fatal casualties, 2 houses demolished), Carlton Road and Stanley Avenue.
12.5 a.m.—H.E.'s near Waverley Crescent and Straight Road.
12.20 a.m.—H.E. between Main Road and Lodge Avenue.
13th/14th 9.35 p.m.—H.E., Main Road/Links Avenue.
3.30 a.m.—H.E., North Street.
15th ... 2.50 p.m.—British Plane crashed near Lodge Lane—pilot uninjured.
16th ... 2.10 a.m.—H.E.'s near Priory, Noak Hill.
17th ... 12.5 a.m.—H.E.'s, Collier Row Lane and Cedar Road.
12.15 a.m.—H.E.'s, Park End Road (1 fatal casualty, 2 houses demolished), and Cross Road (2 houses demolished).
4.30 a.m.—H.E.'s, Lynwood Drive/Clockhouse Lane.
4.50 a.m.—H.E.'s, Eastern Avenue/Mawney Road; H.E.'s north of London Road.
18th ... 2.0 a.m.—Oil Bombs, Pretoria Road/Marks Road, Wheatsheaf Road and Eastern Road.
18th/19th 10.15 p.m.—H.E.'s, Straight Road/Lower Bedfords Road, and Broxhill Road.
12.1 a.m.—H.E.'s on Maylands.
1.20 a.m.—H.E.'s, Bower Farm, Havering.
19th ... 10.0 p.m.—H.E.'s north of Colchester Road.
10.4 p.m.—H.E.'s near Heath Drive.
10.30 p.m.—H.E.'s and Oil Bombs, Upper Bedfords Farm.

People were in their Anderson shelter, just behind the fence on the right, when these two houses in Hill Grove were destroyed on August 10/11th, 1940. One of the houses is the mass of rubble in the foreground.

Devastation in Randall Road at midday on August 30th, 1940.

The rescued piano still plays after the destruction of homes in McIntosh Road on September 10th, 1940.

Three people were killed when a direct hit was made on this house in Havering Drive on September 11th, 1940.

20th ... 11.50 p.m.—H.E.'s, Oaklands Avenue (house demolished), Kingston Road, Carlton Parade, Main Road and Havering Drive (4 fatal casualties. 2 houses demolished).

21st ... 11.35 p.m.—Parachute Mine, Stanley Avenue/Carlton Road (17 houses demolished).

22nd/23rd 8.50 p.m.—H.E.'s and Oil Bombs, Dagenham Road and Old-church Road.

10.50 p.m.—H.E., Heaton Avenue.

11.15 p.m.—H.E., Hornchurch Road (1 fatal casualty, 3 houses demolished).

12.51 a.m.—H.E., Lower Bedfords Road/Straight Road.

3.40 a.m.—H.E., Beauly Way (1 fatal casualty, 2 houses demolished).

23rd ... 9.40 p.m.—Oil Bomb, Noak Hill.

10.20 p.m.—H.E. and Oil Bomb at Havering.

11.30 p.m.—Unexploded Parachute Mine, Birkbeck Road (sub-sequently removed to Bedfords Park and ex-ploded).

11.59 p.m.—H.E.'s near Crichton Gardens.

24th ... 9.50 p.m.—H.E.'s, Hilldene Farm, Straight Road.

29th ... 11.55 p.m.—Oil Bombs, Clockhouse Lane.

30th ... 10.50 p.m.—H.E.'s near Bedfords Park.

OCTOBER, 1940

2nd/3rd 5.10 a.m.—H.E.'s, Faircross Avenue, Erith Crescent (2 houses demolished), Hulse Avenue (2 houses demolished), and White Hart Lane (house demolished)—1 fatal casualty.

4th/5th 9.0 p.m.—Oil Bombs, Bedfords Park ; H.E.'s, Pyrgo Park.

5th/6th 8.30 p.m.—Oil Bomb, Rush Green Road.

10.50 p.m.—H.E.'s, Panmar Avenue (3 houses demolished), Fontayne Avenue and Eastern Avenue/Ashmour Gardens.

12.40 a.m.—H.E.'s, north of Lodge Lane.

1.15 a.m.—H.E.'s, Gidea Park Station area (goods yard and station damaged), Woodfield Drive, Lodge Avenue (4 houses demolished), and Kingston Road.

6th ... 3.0 p.m.—H.E.'s and Oil Bombs near Gidea Park Station, Crossways and Compton Avenue (2 houses demolished).

8th/9th 8.0 p.m.—H.E.'s at Maylands and Dagnam Park.

9.3 p.m.—H.E. near Hainault Road.

9.10 p.m.—H.E.'s near Collier Row Road.

12.27 a.m.—H.E., Paternoster Row, Noak Hill.

3.17 a.m.—H.E.'s at Peek's Farm, Noak Hill.

9th/10th 10.25 p.m.—H.E.'s at Greyhound Stadium and near Crown Hotel, London Road.

8.50 a.m.—H.E.'s, Marlborough Road and Eastern Avenue West (two cars involved in latter incident, with 1 fatal casualty).

10th/11th 8.40 p.m.—H.E.'s, Victoria Road, rear of Town Hall, The Chase (2 houses demolished), Eastern Avenue (house demolished), Ashmour Gardens (2 houses demolished), Horndon Road and Lodge Lane.

10.50 p.m.—H.E.'s, Broxhill Road and Bedfords Park.

11.58 p.m.—H.E.'s between Broxhill Road and Orange Tree Hill.

11th/12th 8.45 p.m.—H.E. near Clockhouse Lane School.
10.45 p.m.—H.E. behind St. Edward's School, Market Place.

13th/14th 8.45 p.m.—H.E. near " White Hart," Collier Row Road.
9.0 p.m.—Oil Bombs at Oldchurch Hospital, The Brewery, the Telephone Exchange and North Street (large Store burnt out).
9.40 p.m.—H.E.'s, Netherpark Drive (3 houses demolished).
9.45 p.m.—H.E.'s, Horndon Road/Saffron Road and Cross Road.

15th/16th 10.0 p.m.—H.E.'s and Oil Bombs, George Street (5 houses demolished), Randall Road (4 houses demolished), Kingston Road (2 houses demolished), and Richmond Road.
10.15 p.m.—H.E.'s in and near Lodge Avenue.
10.35 p.m.—H.E.'s, Sheila Close, Carter Drive, Ramsden Drive, Lynwood Drive, Larchwood Avenue, Dominion Drive (1 house demolished), Riversdale Road (3 houses demolished), Collier Row Road, and White Hart Lane.

16th/17th 7.35 p.m.—H.E., Pettits Lane.
7.40 p.m.—Two Parachute Mines in Havering Village (4 houses demolished).
8.10 p.m.—H.E.'s in and near Lawns Way and The Drive (5 fatal casualties).
10.20 p.m.—H.E.'s, Lower Bedfords Road and Pyrgo Park.
11.30 p.m.—H.E.'s, Richards Avenue (house demolished), Recreation Avenue (5 houses demolished), Knightsbridge Gardens, London Road, and Cottons Recreation Ground (shelter hit—6 fatal casualties).

18th/19th 8.10 p.m.—H.E.'s and Oil Bombs south of Lower Bedfords Road.

20th/21st 10.10 p.m.—H.E.'s and Oil Bombs, Beauly Way, Park Boulevard, Heath Drive (1 house demolished), Gidea Close and Eastern Avenue (West).
11.45 p.m.—H.E.'s north of Carter Drive.
11.50 p.m.—H.E.'s, Birkbeck Road and Wolseley Road.
12.35 a.m.—H.E., Pyrgo Park.

21st/22nd 7.45 p.m.—H.E.'s near Round House, Havering.
9.50 p.m.—H.E., Hornchurch Road.

23rd/24th 10.45 p.m.—H.E.'s, High Street, London Road (house demolished), Pettley Gardens, Marina Gardens, rear Marks Road, and Weald Way/Stanford Close.
1.30 a.m.—H.E.'s, Crow Lane.

24th/25th 8.20 p.m.—H.E.'s and Oil Bombs, Berkeley Avenue, Lawnsway (house demolished), Hillfoot Avenue, Erith Crescent, and Chase Cross Road (2 fatal casualties),
Just after noon on the 25th—British plane crashed near Woodstock Avenue.

28th/29th p.m.—H.E.'s south of Collier Row Road.

29th/30th 2.10 a.m.—H.E.'s in and near Chase Cross Road.

30th ... 9.25 p.m.—H.E. at Noak Hill.
9.50 p.m.—H.E.'s, Marks Road (4 houses demolished), Richards Avenue and Oak Street.
10.0 p.m.—H.E.'s in Wolseley Road and Rush Green Road.

31st ... 7.50 p.m.—H.E.'s in and near Carter Drive.

24

A sea of destruction at Romford Brewery on April 19th, 1941, as a result of an incendiary raid. The Brewery was damaged on five separate occasions during the war.

Havering Road School Hall, wrecked on
November 30th, 1940.

1st ... 7.0 p.m.—H.E., Mashiters Walk; H.E.'s and Oil Bombs, Pettits Lane School and between Beauly Way and Eastern Avenue.

9.25 p.m.—H.E.'s and Oil Bombs, Main Road/Heath Drive (1 fatal casualty, 1 house demolished), Broadway and Park Boulevard.

2nd ... 10.0 p.m.—H.E.'s in and near Waverley Crescent, and Straight Road.

4th/5th 7.55 p.m.—Nineteen unexploded H.E.'s in a line from Lodge Avenue to Crow Lane, falling (among other places) in South Street, on the L.N.E.R., and on the Gas Works.

3.45 a.m.—H.E.'s in Bedfords Park.

5.0 a.m.—H.E.'s at Upper Bedfords Farm.

5.20 a.m.—H.E.'s near Straight Road.

6th ... 7.5 p.m.—H.E., Recreation Avenue.

11.15 p.m.—H.E., Yew Tree Gardens.

11.20 p.m.—H.E.'s, Rush Green Road, near Birkbeck Road and in the Cemetery.

8th/9th 8.33 p.m.—H.E. north of Colchester Road.

2.0 a.m.—Thirteen unexploded H.E.'s in Dagnam Park

9th ... 10.0 p.m.—H.E. at Upper Bedfords Farm

10th ... 7.50 p.m.—H.E.'s near Links Avenue

8.0 p.m.—H.E.'s, Heaton Close (2 houses demolished), Tennyson Road and Straight Road

10.25 p.m.—H.E.'s at Noak Hill

11.0 p.m.—H.E.'s and Oil Bombs, Havering Park Farm

13th ... 6.55 p.m.—H.E.'s in Hamilton Avenue (2 houses demolished), Ashmour Gardens, Eastern Avenue, North Street, and on Havering Road School

15th ... 10.55 p.m.—H.E.'s near Hog Hill Road and Collier Row Road

16th ... 7.30 p.m.—H.E. north of Colchester Road

10.30 p m —Three Parachute Mines, Havering Park Farm and Bower Farm, Havering

20th ... 5 30 a.m.—H.E.'s near Church Road, Noak Hill.

6.10 a.m.—H.E.'s at Bower Farm, Havering, and Clockhouse Lane.

24th ... 9.25 p.m.—Mine, Cedric Avenue (5 fatal casualties, 10 houses demolished).

30th ... 12.5 a.m.—H.E., Romford Golf Course.

DECEMBER, 1940

3rd ... 8.25 p.m.—Ten H.E.'s between London Road and Collier Row Road.

8th/9th 10.50 p.m.—H.E., Havering Park Farm.

11.0 p.m.—Parachute Mine, Oldchurch Road (2 fatal casualties, 2 houses, Civil Defence Depot and Mortuary demolished); H.E.'s, Beechfield Gardens, Grosvenor Road (1 house demolished), and on Gasworks.

11.10 p.m.—Parachute Mine, Exchange Street (2 shops demolished, Telephone Exchange partly demolished, 2 fatal casualties); H.E.'s, Jubilee Avenue and Cromer Road.

11.14 p.m.—Parachute Mine north of Colchester Road.

DECEMBER, 1940 (continued)

8th/9th
(contd).
    11.15 p.m.—H.E.'s, Sheringham Avenue, Rush Green Road (house demolished), and the Cemetery.

    12.5 a.m.—H.E.'s, St. John's Road and Clockhouse Lane.

    1.0 a.m.—Delayed action H.E.'s, Belle Vue Road and Mount Pleasant Road.

    1.10 a.m.—H.E.'s, Stanley Avenue and Woodfield Drive; H.E.'s, Collier Row Lane, Collier Row Road and Carlton Road.

    1.20 a.m.—Magnesium Incendiaries, Havering Park and Clockhouse Lane School.

    1.55 a.m.—H.E., Meadow Road (2 fatal casualties, 2 houses demolished).

22nd ... 5.50 p.m.—H.E.'s west of Meadow Road.

27th ... 8.0 p.m.—Parachute Mine, Balgores Lane (7 houses demolished); Unexploded Parachute Mine, Balgores Lane/Stanley Avenue; H.E., Hillfoot Road.

    10.0 p.m.—Tarboid Incendiary near North Street.

29th ... 7.40 p.m.—H.E.'s near 305, London Road.

JANUARY, 1941

5th ... 7.45 p.m.—H.E.'s, Pinewood Road.

    8.30 p.m.—H.E.'s. Upper Bedfords Farm.

    9.10 p.m.—H.E. near Heaton Avenue.

    9.25 p.m.—H.E.'s, Beech Street, Cedar Road, Western Road and South Street.

    9.30 p.m.—H.E.'s, Albert Road, east of Romford Station, Milton Road, Linden Street, Como Street (2 houses demolished), and Linden Street/Mawney Road.

7th ... 12.40 p.m.—H.E.'s between Rush Green Road and Crow Lane.

12th ... 9.30 p.m.—H.E.'s at Maylands, Gravel Pits Oldchurch Road, and Colchester Road (2 houses demolished).

29th ... 7.47 p.m.—H.E., Wrightsbridge Road, Noak Hill.

FEBRUARY, 1941

5th ... 8.25 p.m.—H.E.'s, Lodge Avenue, rear of Victoria Hospital Woodlands Road (2 houses demolished), Pettits Lane and Lowshoe Lane.

26th ... 9.45 p.m.—H.E., Pettits Lane/Heather Gardens.

    10.10 p.m.—H.E.'s, Dagnam Park.

MARCH, 1941

9th .;. 9.10 p.m.—H.E., Wolseley Road (5 fatal casualties, 17 houses demolished).

15th ... 8.50 p.m.—300–400 Explosive Incendiaries over a wide area.

    10.45 p.m.—H.E.'s, Oldchurch Hospital (Doctor's block and Offices demolished), Crow Lane/Oldchurch Road, and Coombewood Drive; Incendiaries in London Road and Crow Lane area.

18th ... 4.20 a.m.—H.E.'s, Ramsden Drive, Carter Drive, Carter Close, (1 house demolished), Collier Row Road and Lodge Lane (1 fatal casualty).

APRIL, 1941

19th/20th
    9.40 p.m.—Parachute Mine, Essex Road (38 fatal casualties, 17 houses demolished).

    9.45 p.m.—H.E.'s, Netherpark Drive (4 houses demolished).

    10.15 p.m.—Parachute Mine, Hillfoot Avenue (6 fatal casualties 22 houses demolished).

26

When the "Squirrel's Head," Squirrels Heath, was badly blasted on May 10th, 1941, the motto was "Business as usual." On the morning following the raid, customers arrived and were served as if nothing had happened, though the ceilings, windows and fittings had been smashed.

A family of three was rescued alive from this Anderson shelter in Albert Road, near which a bomb fell.

This picture shows what remained of All Saints' Parochial Hall, Squirrels Heath, after the parachute mine explosion on May 11th, 1941.

APRIL, 1941 (continued)

19th/20th (*contd.*) 10.30 p.m.—Parachute Mine between Carlisle Road and Princes Road (35 houses demolished).

10.45 p.m.—Parachute Mine, Pettits Lane (15 houses demolished).
11.0 p.m.—Parachute Mine near Crown Cottages, London Road.
12.25 a.m.—Incendiaries near Oldchurch Road.
12.30 a.m.—H.E., Havering Park Farm.
2.20 a.m.—Parachute Mine near White Hart Lane ; Parachute Mine near Eastern Avenue (West).
3.0 a.m.—Parachute Mine near Lodge Lane.

MAY, 1941

10th ... 4.10 a.m.—H.E.'s, Dagnam Park.
11th ... 12.45 a.m.—Parachute Mine, Upper Brentwood Road (All Saints Church and 16 houses demolished) ; Parachute Mine, Castellan Avenue (1 fatal casualty, 8 houses demolished).

2.20 a.m.—H.E., Harrow Crescent.
18th ... 12.12 a.m.—Incendiaries, Rush Green.

JULY, 1941

28th ... 2.45 a.m.—H.E.'s, Catherine Road and Hamilton Road (1 fatal casualty, 4 houses demolished).

1943

12th March ... 7.40 a.m.—Machine-gun attack by enemy planes.
15th June ... 1.50 a.m.—H.E.'s, Park Farm, Havering.
7th October ... 10.0 p.m.—H.E.'s, Romford Golf Course.
8th November 10.41 p.m.—H.E.'s near Pinewood Road and Wellingtonia Avenue (1 house demolished).
26th November 9.25 p.m.—H.E. between Lodge Lane and Carter Drive.

1944

22nd January 5.20 a.m.—Incendiaries, Albert Road/Victoria Road area (1 fatal casualty) ; and in High Street area (Bottling Dept. at Brewery badly damaged).
3rd February 10.50 p.m.—German plane crashed between Lower Bedfords Road and Havering Road (North).
19th February 1.09 a.m.—H.E., North Road, Havering.
20th February 10.10 p.m.—H.E. between Rosedale Road and Hainault Road.

10.15 p.m.—H.E.'s, Lodge Lane and Havering Park Farm.
24th February 10.0 p.m.—H.E.'s, Collier Row Road and Lynwood Drive.
19th April ... 1.5 a.m.—Incendiary Bombs in High Street, London Road and Collier Row area (1 fatal casualty, 12 houses and shops destroyed, Allen's Garage, London Road, destroyed ; Havering Road School damaged).
16th June ... 2.25 a.m.—Fly Bomb, Collier Row Road, near Whalebone Lane.

3.30 a.m.—Fly Bomb, Barton Avenue (7 fatal casualties, 18 houses demolished).
17th June ... 5.27 a.m.—Fly Bomb, Lodge Lane (1 fatal casualty, 12 houses demolished).
21st June ... 5.0 a.m.—Fly Bomb, Hainault Road (3 fatal casualties 15 houses demolished).

1944 (continued)

22nd June	...	4.10 a.m.—Fly Bomb near Heaton Way.
23rd June	...	6.56 a.m.—Fly Bomb, Parkland Avenue.
25th June	...	1.40 a.m.—Fly Bomb, Fowlers Farm, Collier Row Road.
		9.50 p.m.—Fly Bomb, Clockhouse Lane (2 fatal casualties, 10 houses demolished).
30th June	...	8.12 p.m.—Fly Bomb on L.N.E.R., east of Romford Station.
1st July	...	11.55 p.m.—Fly Bomb, north-west of Lodge Farm, Lodge Lane.
4th July	...	9.19 p.m.—Fly Bomb between 'Eastern Avenue and Marlborough Road.
8th July	...	12.30 a.m.—Fly Bomb, Mawney Road/Percy Road (1 fatal casualty, 11 houses demolished).
23rd July	...	12.30 a.m.—Fly Bomb just north of Gallows Corner.
27th July	...	5.40 p.m.—Fly Bomb between Havering Road and Lower Bedfords Road.
5th August	...	7.20 a.m.—Fly Bomb between Gorseway and Rush Green Road (5 fatal casualties, 16 houses demolished).
6th August	...	11.20 p.m.—Fly Bomb, Hillfoot Road/Collier Row Lane (1 fatal casualty, 14 houses demolished).
7th August	...	7.30 a.m.—Fly Bomb, Bower Farm, Havering.
12th August	...	6.25 a.m.—Fly Bomb north of Noak Hill Road (1 house demolished).
28th August	...	12.59 a.m.—Fly Bomb at Havering Park Farm.
16th September		—Rocket in Wrightsbridge Road, Noak Hill.
5th October	...	7.58 p.m.—Fly Bomb, Benskins Lane, Noak Hill.
4th November		—Rocket, Lower Bedfords Road.
5th November		—Rocket, west of Cross Road.
12th November		—Rocket, south of Noak Hill Road.
13th November		—Rocket in Dagenham Road (in Dagenham area) damaged property in Romford.
15th November		—Rocket, Ainsley Avenue (8 houses demolished).
16th November		—Rocket, Collier Row Lane/Rosedale Road (13 fatal casualties, 34 houses demolished).
31st December		—Rocket west of Meadow Road.
		—Rocket, Chequers Road, Noak Hill.

1945

16th January	...	—Rocket, Broxhill Road/Noak Hill Road.
21st January	...	—Rocket, Dagnam Park, Noak Hill.
11th February		—Rocket, south of Collier Row Road.
14th February		—Rocket, Pyrgo Park, Havering.
		—Rocket in Bedfords Park.
20th February		—Rocket, Fairholme Avenue (12 fatal casualties, 8 houses demolished).
22nd February		—Rocket, west of Cross Road.
2nd March	...	—Rocket, Wellingtonia Avenue, Havering.
4th March	...	—Rocket, south-west of Liberty Cottages, Havering (1 house demolished).
8th March	...	—Rocket, north of Colchester Road.
14th March	...	—Rocket, Havering Park Farm.
21st March	...	—Rocket exploded overhead—turbine and other parts fell in Ferguson Avenue, Edward Close and near Harrow Crescent.
26th March	...	—Rocket, Mawney Road/Forest Road (2 fatal casualties, 16 houses demolished).
		—Rocket at Noak Hill (Victory Hut demolished).

28

The rocking horse came to the surface when a large house at the corner of Heath Drive and Main Road, Gidea Park, was completely demolished on November 1st, 1940. One person in the house was killed.

Smashed houses in Havering Road—the result of a rocket on June 21st, 1944.

Another view of the damage in Collier Row Lane, caused by the rocket on November 15th, 1944.

Wrecked houses in Jutsums Lane as a result of an "incident" on November 15th, 1944.

ROLL OF HONOUR

CIVILIAN FATAL CASUALTIES

1940

CEDRIC ATKINSON.
DONALD ATKINSON.
ELLY ATKINSON.
MABEL BARKER.
WILLIAM H. G. BARKER.
ARTHUR M. BEATTIE (16 years).
WILLIAM S. BURCHNALL.
ALAN CHIPP (11 months).
ANN E. CHIPP (2 years).
CHARLOTTE M. CHIPP.
JEAN D. CHIPP (4 years).
JOHN W. R. CHIPP.
EDITH COLE.
ALAN C. COLE (1 year)
TERENCE H. G. COLE (5 years).
EDWIN COPPING.
ALFRED S. CRABB.
CONSTANCE M. DIBLEY.
ARTHUR C. ELLIS (4 years).
WALTER C. ELLIS.

EDWARD FLEMING.
MARGERITA GONELLA.
WILLIAM HARRINGTON.
ARTHUR H. MINTER (10 years).
WALTER J. PEARSON.
CATHERINE PLUMMER.
ELSIE PLUMMER.
HERBERT PLUMMER.
JOHN R. POLLARD.
GERALD B. RYCRAFT.
KATHLEEN M. RYCRAFT.
PETER B. RYCRAFT (15 years).
WALTER G. RYCRAFT.
ADA SMITH.
ANN P. SMITH (2 years).
FREDERICK STEVENS (5 years).
WILLIAM A. TRIMNELL.
PERCY A. VANGO.
JAMES W. WARREN.
SARAH E. WARREN.
ALICE M. WHITE.

1941

ERNEST BARCLAY.
GORDON BARCLAY.
JOHN BARCLAY.
MARY BEATRICE BARCLAY.
PHYLLIS BARCLAY.
JOAN BEAN.
RICHARD BEDFORD.
FRANCIS G. BIXBY (12 years).
ELIZABETH CARTER.
VERA CARTER (10 years).
BARBARA LIMEHOUSE (5 years).
BERYL LIMEHOUSE (11 years).
EDWIN LIMEHOUSE (10 years).
EDWIN LIMEHOUSE (Senior).
MAUD LIMEHOUSE.
DONALD A. W. MAYES (4 years).
EDITH E. R. MAYES.
JOHN MAYES (2 years).
DAVID R. QUINCEY (1 year).
VIOLETTA M. K. QUINCEY.
PATHANEY RATCLIFFE.
RHODA A. REEKS.
ROSINA R. REEKS (9 years).
LESLIE W. RIDINGTON (10 months).
ELIZABETH SIMMONS.

GEORGINA CHESTER (4 years).
MARY A. CHESTER.
ELSIE DENNIS (14 years).
LILY DENNIS (16 years).
GEORGE W. DUNCAN.
LOUISA ELLIS.
ROSINA HOBBS.
CHARLES J. HOLLANDS.
DAISY JOLLEY.
FLORENCE I. LEWIS.
ERNEST H. THOMAS.
JOSEPHINE TRACEY.
MARGARET TRACEY.
CAROL WALLING (2 years).
MAY E. WALLING.
WALTER H. WHITTAKER.
JOYCE I. WILSON (7 years).
ROY WILSON (5 years).
THOMAS S. WILSON.
WINIFRED I. WILSON.
DORIS HELEN WOOD.
HENRY WOOD.
JAMES WOOD.
ROBERT WOOD.

1944

Adeline ATTWOOD.
Alan BARNES (7 years).
Beatrice BARNES.
Florence A. COPSEY.
Leonard Keith COPSEY (8 years).
Beatrice CRAY.
Barbara CROWE (1 year).
Beatrice CROWE.
Maureen CROWE (7 years).
John EARL (13 years).
Minnie EARL.
Ronald EARL (11 years).
Anthony ELLIOTT (12 years).
May ELLIOTT.
Harold FULCHER.
Kenneth HARBURN.
Ivy KEY.
Maureen KEY.

Clara KINCH.
Blanche LARNER.
Arthur LITTLE.
Susannah LITTLE.
Betty MITCHELL (16 years).
Lilian MITCHELL.
Alexandra MOORHOUSE.
John E. ROBERTS.
Eileen SARGEANT (10 years).
Emily SARGEANT.
George W. SARGEANT.
Annie SELLEN.
Alice E. SHARP.
Alice TIZZARD.
Charles TUBBY.
Queenie WALLACE.
Edith WEMBRIDGE.
Lily E. WHITEMAN.

1945

George BARNETT.
Lilian L. BARTLEY.
Sophia BARTLEY.
William F. BARTLEY.
Ellen CARTER.
Iris HALLAS.
Lilian E. HITCHCOCK.

John L. HUGHES.
Keith JONES.
Arthur NORRIS.
Sidney G. TURNER.
Barbara A. WEST (14 years).
David H. WEST (7 years).
John L. WEST (10 years).

CIVIL DEFENCE ORGANISATION

It is a little difficult in this year and after we have had two VE-days of celebration following the cessation of hostilities in Europe and two VJ-days to denote our victory over the Japanese, to remember precisely the beginning of Civil Defence in Romford. There are records to which reference can be made but it is not desired to fill this volume with statistics, but simply to give a general picture of Romford's part in the war which started in September, 1939.

From 1935 onwards, the Government had warned Local Authorities of the necessity to do something in connection with Civil Defence, and to prepare what was then called an " A.R.P. Scheme." In so far as Romford was concerned, the authority responsible for such a Scheme was the Essex County Council, and Romford's Scheme was an integral part of the County's proposals. The Romford Council took the matter seriously, and from the beginning appreciated that Romford's close proximity to London would undoubtedly expose the town to a considerable amount of attention by the enemy.

The Council from time to time considered Air-Raid Precautions as they then understood them, and in February, 1938, appointed an A.R.P. Committee, the first meeting of which was held on March 15th, 1938. It is interesting to note that at that meeting matters were discussed such as the Fire Patrol Scheme, the appointment of an Air-Raid Precautions Officer, the enrolment of personnel, the reservation of vehicles, and the completion of the A.R.P. Scheme for Romford. The Committee further decided at its first meeting to invite applications from public-spirited townsfolk to enrol as volunteers in the A.R.P. Scheme, and Air-Raid Shelters were also the subject of consideration.

September, 1938, brought with it the Munich crisis, and matters began to take on a more serious colour and a greater urgency.

With the help of the volunteers who had already enrolled, respirators, or, as they were known then, and as they still are known, gas masks, were distributed to the public at various centres throughout the town. Some 62,000 were purchased and handed to the public in boxes after they had been fitted by members of the Wardens' Service.

In September, 1938, also the Council got busy on shelters. They discussed the merits of deep shelters and of surface shelters, and by September, 1939, there was public shelter accommodation in the town for seating approximately 4,500 people.

31

The A.R.P. Committee continued to meet monthly and at more frequent intervals when necessary up to September 3rd, 1939, when, with the invasion of Poland, the Government declared war with Germany. Then it was necessary to give, not only primary but complete attention to Air-Raid Precautions, and for the most part the normal Council work was suspended, and every available officer and workman turned over to A.R.P. work. The Council set up an Emergency Committee which, for the first month of the war, met almost daily, and afterwards met as and when required, which meant that it assembled at very frequent intervals. All committees were suspended, and such matters as had to be dealt with were referred to the Emergency Committee. The Council was in a difficulty—it was met by an astounding shortage of the necessary materials, for A.R.P. work, and furthermore, it had to ask the County Council for authority to expend money on Air-Raid Precautions. In many cases, the County themselves could not deal with the matter and had to communicate with the Eastern Region, and Eastern Region at times had to refer to Whitehall. The times were stern and the need urgent, so that things were done which were without precedent in Local Government, but they were all done with one intention and one motive only, and that, the safety of the people of Romford. Romford was in no worse position than any other town in the country, but its inhabitants felt—and future events showed that they were correct—that they were in the front line, and that it was imperative that their Air-Raid Precautions should be as perfect as it was possible for them to be. The black-out, which was to last for nearly six years, became operative throughout the Borough, and it became the duty of every occupier of premises to prevent the escape of any light from their buildings. This was no easy task, and many very worthy citizens found themselves being reprimanded or fined because of some small accident or oversight in connection with this matter which, of necessity, was strictly enforced.

MANY VOLUNTEERS

Romford was fortunate in the number of volunteers who gave their services to Civil Defence, and it says much for their local patriotism that a large majority of them remained as volunteers in the Civil Defence Service throughout the period of the war, and did not consider themselves as demobilised from their duties until May 2nd, 1945, brought with it the " Stand-down " of Civil Defence. Members of the Council gave of their time and abilities ; one of them assisted in the purchase of second-hand cars for transport purposes, another acted as an honorary A.R.P. Inspector, a third became Deputy County A.R.P. Controller, and others joined the Wardens' Service and other branches of the Civil Defence Services. Councillor G. F. Chaplin became in July,

1940, the A.R.P. Controller, succeeding an official of the Council in this office. At the same time, Alderman W. J. Russell was appointed Deputy Controller. Unfortunately, Councillor Chaplin was unable, owing to ill-health, to function as Controller, and in December, 1940, after having fulfilled the major function for some months, Alderman W. J. Russell, J.P., was formally promoted from Deputy to Controller. Alderman Russell's connection with and interest in Civil Defence continued to its " Stand-down " in May, 1945, and his services as Controller or County Sub-Controller having been at Romford's disposal throughout the whole of the period from 1940 to 1945.

It is difficult to explain the ramifications of Civil Defence in Romford so as to make it clear to the average citizen how Civil Defence worked, but that it did work, and satisfactorily, is beyond dispute. Never once during the 5¾ years of its existence did it break down, and this in spite of the fact that there were 1,264 alerts sounded during that period.

The first alert was on September 3rd, 1939, less than an hour after the country had been told of the declaration of war. At the hub of the Civil Defence services in Romford, namely, the Report Centre, in the basement of the Town Hall, everyone seemed to be ready, and expecting something to happen, but fortunately nothing did. The preparations were at that time not in the best of shape, and it was well that there were a number of, shall, we say, inoperative alerts before Civil Defence had to settle down to its real business.

The Town Hall was a new building, completed in 1937, and it had to be pulled about in order to provide for such an extra as a Report Centre. But it must be agreed that the strong rooms which had been constructed in the basement of the building provided very suitable Report Centre accommodation. One of the rooms in the basement was converted into a Control Room, another into a Telephonists' Room, a third was placed at the disposal of the Heads of the various Services for consultation purposes, and a fourth was converted into sleeping accommodation by the intruduction of bunks. The Report Centre personnel made a habit of smoking while they were on duty, and, not surprisingly, having regard to the nervous tension induced by war conditions, this habit grew, and the atmosphere was often somewhat cloudy. But the difficult conditions through the lack of comfort and, in the early years, of subsistence, did not detract from the camaraderie which existed all during the war in the Report Centre nor from the efficiency with which it worked.

The Report Centre was manned very largely by volunteers, and, in fact, during the last two years almost entirely by voluntary assistance. Three of the shifts were, during the whole of the period of the war, provided by local youth organisations, whose assistance was very much appreciated.

In the Report Centre also were the Controller, the Borough Engineer, the Medical Officer of Health, and representatives of the Public Utility Undertakings, namely, the South Essex Waterworks Company, the County of London Electric Supply Co., Ltd., and the Romford Gas Company. These Companies were most helpful in their attendance in the Report Centre and in their subsequent speed and efficiency in repairing services damaged by enemy action. Their representation in the Report Centre enabled them to obtain immediate information of war damage, and they were able, without delay, to repair the damage and reinstate the services. There were very few cases in the town where people were without a supply of water or of electricity or gas for any considerable period, despite the fact that the damage done was often widespread and fraught with considerable difficulty.

Again, in the Report Centre was a representative of the Auxiliary Fire Service (later the National Fire Service), and there was a direct telephone to the Police Station, as well as to the Mawney Road Fire Station.

In the Report Centre itself members of the Council's staffs helped in the rota of duties and attended during the difficult times when the other volunteers were unable to be present, often in addition to their own voluntary regular duty. The Report Centre owed much to the Town Hall staff.

To provide the Report Centre with the information which it required, there were 43 Wardens' Posts throughout the Borough, and from these Wardens' Posts was telephoned immediately it was available, information as to any and every incident which occurred. Some of the " incidents " were really not incidents arising from enemy action at all, and to some extent the Report Centre was used as a kind of clearing house for matters of extreme urgency, but whatever messages were received were dealt with in good faith and as quickly and efficiently as was practicable. When the Report Centre was able to judge the magnitude of any incident, its duty was then to order out the necessary Rescue Parties, Ambulances, First-Aid Parties, Road Repair Parties, etc., and to keep the County Control Centre informed of the progress of events in the Borough, the amount of Services still available in the Council's Depots, and the possibility of Romford having to request the County to provide mutual help from other Civil Defence Centres in the County. There were a few times when the Report Centre was deluged with reports to such an extent that it could not deal with all of them immediately, and it had then to select those which were felt to be the most important, and to leave the others to be dealt with later.

The Wardens' Service which was for the major part of the war period administered directly by the Essex County Police, was an organisation formidable in personnel. It was, of course, part of the Town's Civil Defence Services and operationally came under the direction of Romford's A.R.P. Sub-Controller. It functioned from Posts throughout the Borough and was the " eye " of the Report Centre. Its members will remember the report forms which they had to use and which caused as much annoyance to them as they did to the Report Centre. But the reports came through and though at times they could not give all the details needed by County Control, they served to convey sufficient information to enable the required services to be despatched. Great credit is due to the members of the Wardens' Service for their untiring nightly vigils in very uncongenial surroundings.

In close connection with the Wardens' Service, Romford had the assistance of the County Police and of the Police Reserve. Superintendent O. Knights was in charge of the Romford Division throughout the War and he did his war work with the efficiency which we in Romford have become so used to expect from him and the officers and men under his control. Towards the end of the war, Superintendent Knights was awarded the King's Police Medal in recognition of his leadership. Mr. W. G. Comfort succeeded Mr. A. B. Rowe as Chief Warden for the Borough and remained in office until the " Stand Down " of the Wardens' Service.

Attached also to the Report Centre were the volunteer Incident Officers who, when requested so to do, went out in the dark and often in the rain and snow to control the services sent to incidents. There were also available Gas Identification Officers whose services, fortunately, never had to be called upon in actual operations.

The Rescue Parties and the First-aid Parties carried out their work sympathetically and efficiently. At times they were working 24 hours at a stretch—at other times they were just waiting for something to happen. When at an incident they would work furiously on the debris heaving masses of rubble away, but became as gentle as any nurse when having reached their objective, they started to remove the buried victim. Their joy at each " live " rescue was manifest and their sympathetic handling of distressed relatives who would try to help was wonderful to see. The public in Romford who, unfortunately, suffered as a result of enemy action, have nothing but praise for the manner in which they carried out their work. There was a Mobile First-aid Unit stationed at one of the Depots which proved very efficient in use, and provided immediate medical attention on the scenes of many incidents.

At the outbreak of war, there were three Civil Defence Depots, one in the Town Yard, Market Place, another in Havering Road, and a third in Oldchurch Road, but the last named was later destroyed by enemy action, and was replaced by the Depot in Cottons Recreation Ground.

Again, at the outbreak of war, there were five First-aid Posts, these being respectively situate at Oldchurch Hospital, St. Michael's Hall, London Road School, Victoria Hospital and Clockhouse Lane School, but at the stand-down of Civil Defence we find that this number was reduced to two, namely, those at St. Michael's Hall and in Clockhouse Lane School. The Depots and Posts were manned night and day for over five-years.

There were times when the telephone service ceased to function owing to enemy action. These were difficult and onerous periods for the Report Centre which depended so much for its information and also for the despatch of its instructions on the telephone service. However, a band of youthful cyclists was available, and this, the Messenger Service, functioned throughout the war with its headquarters in the Report Centre. Until the stand-down of Civil Defence a rota of Messengers was provided nightly in the Report Centre. These lads so often had nothing to do, and it must be said to their credit that in spite of the many eventless periods which they spent on duty in the Report Centre, they were never wanting when they were needed for some job. When the telephones were not available they proved invaluable, and at other times through the war period they carried messages and performed many other tasks which the Report Centre required of them. It can well be said of the Messenger Service " They also serve who only stand and wait."

The occurrence of incidents in the Borough proved, of course, the necessity for further Services. The injured had to be taken to Oldchurch Hospital or to First-Aid Posts, the homeless had to be provided with accommodation in Rest Centres, the dead were taken to the Council's Civil Defence Mortuary.

Oldchurch Hospital dealt not only with casualties from Romford, but also those from Hornchurch, Dagenham, Ilford and Barking, and even from further afield, and much could be written about the efficiency of the medical and nursing staff, and the kindness and courtesy meted out to those unfortunate residents who had to be taken to Oldchurch Hospital for treatment. Never once during the war period did the Hospital find itself unable to deal with a casualty.

The Rest Centre Service functioned from Mawney Road, and from a number of other buildings in the Borough, and was controlled by the Essex County Council. With the assistance of a number of ladies, the comfort provided in the Mawney Road Rest Centre was added to by the provision of a Clothing Store which supplemented that provided by the Romford Branch of the W.V.S. Those people, who unfortunately, had to resort to the Rest Centre received every kindness and consideration from the County officials and also from the band of ladies who were always available at the Centre. Mention must be made also of the Sick Bay provided at the Rest Centre and staffed by the Romford Branch of the British Red Cross Society.

The Council Mortuary Service was provided by Council employees and others under the supervision, firstly, of Mr. S. W. Mason, the Parks Superintendent, and latterly, of Mr. W. H. Mott. This was probably the most gruesome part of the Civil Defence Services, and the Mortuary Squads had a delicate and painful task to perform, but they did it to the satisfaction not only of themselves but of the relatives of those folk who lost their lives. Coupled with the dealing with the dead bodies of the persons who were killed was the collection and disposal of personal effects recovered from bodies. This again, was a service which did not obtain much publicity, but it was an integral part of the Council's assistance for families and individuals affected by enemy action. There was also the Casualty Bureau which was set up following each incident and which made information available as to persons who had been killed or injured as a result of an air raid.

The Billeting Officer had an arduous and responsible duty following incidents, but with the use of requisitioned premises it was mainly practicable either to billet or to rehouse families whose houses had been destroyed, and it says much for the efficiency of the services generally that the Rest Centre was never opened for a continuous period of more than four days. In the matter of billeting, the Romford W.V.S. played an important and helpful part. It also assisted, coupled with the Clothing Centre at Mawney Road Rest Centre, in the re-clothing of people who had lost all their clothing as the result of an incident, and much good was done in this direction to maintain the morale of people who appeared to have lost their all by a very near incident.

Later in the war, the " Good Neighbour Scheme," inaugurated by the W.V.S., with the assistance of the then Mayor, Alderman A. J. Dyer, did a wonderful work in providing furniture for Romford people. The furniture was collected by the W.V.S. in other parts of the country, including mainly West Suffolk, Norfolk and Norwich, and was sent to Romford for distribution under a " points " scheme propounded by the W.V.S. In this way bomb-victim families were able to receive such articles as perambulators, cots, cradles and essential items of furniture which were all but unobtainable through the normal trade channels.

Another service in Romford which assisted as an essential part of the Town's Civil Defence, was the Shelter Controllers. In Romford we did not have to face the necessity of employing full-time Controllers, for, as has been mentioned previously, the town was always willing to provide volunteers. In this instance, Mr. E. H. Skinner gave his services and was appointed Hon. Shelter Controller for the Borough. He was assisted by Mr. W. L. Cooke, and by over 150 ladies and gentlemen whose duty it was to see that the public shelters were unlocked and ready for use immediately they were required, and who, further, undertook the serious obligation of seeing that the persons using the shelters behaved themselves, and were made as comfortable as possible. A visit to one of the main shelters late in the evening often made one wonder how people could be happy and contented in such an atmosphere, but nevertheless the comfort of the shelters was such as to render them a boon and a blessing to those people who had no alternative shelter accommodation, and to those who were nervous or who wanted the society of other people during the very extended periods when the Alerts were on. Mr. Skinner and his colleagues provided entertainment, they were responsible for the running of canteens in some of the shelters, and they provided funds for the assistance of indigent shelterers. Further, as part of Mr. Skinner's programme of shelter control, personnel attached to the British Red Cross Society and the St. John Ambulance Brigade provided a rota of attendances at some of the shelters in the centre of the Town, and were always available to give assistance to those shelterers who needed it.

The Home Guard and the Auxiliary Fire Service (afterwards the National Fire Service) while not (with the exception of the Auxiliary Fire Service) under the control of the Corporation, were nevertheless only too anxious and willing to assist the Civil Defence Services. The Home Guard provided during part of the period of the war a nightly guard at the Report Centre when invasion was a matter of speculation, and the 4th Battalion of the Essex Home Guard under Col. P. C. Henderson, and later, of his successors, Lt.-Col. H. B. Pett, Lt.-Col. M. R. W. E. Mount, and Lt.-Col. F. Graham, assisted throughout by Lt.-Col. A. F. Leggett, O.B.E., was most helpful when it came to the question of forming Invasion Committees.

Three Invasion Committees were actually formed, and did some useful preliminary work. One covered the centre of Romford, and was under the Chairmanship of the Mayor for the time being, one was set up for the Collier Row and Havering Area under the chairmanship of Councillor W. D. Hill, and the third, under the guidance of Mr. E. Hammer, dealt with the outlying portion of the Borough in the Noak Hill area.

Members of the Home Guard further were often seen on the scene of incidents assisting the Civil Defence Services in rescue, transport, clearance, and other work. They also proved invaluable in helping the Police to guard chattels in damaged homes until first aid repairs could be completed.

When the German aircraft came along with incendiary bombs, the importance of what was then the Supplementary Fire Parties loomed large. Here again Romford was prepared. Before the Fire Guard Organisation was set up, Mr. S. J. F. Davis, Romford's former captain of the Fire Brigade, prepared a scheme with the assistance of Mr. Sidney H. Smith, as a result of which the major part of the Borough was covered by volunteers known as Supplementary Fire Parties, and when, in September, 1941, the Fire Guard Organisation was officially set up, Romford was in the happy position of having a general scheme already in operation. Many will remember the registrations which took place for fire guard duty, and the horror which filled many of us mere men at the possibility of having women on duty as fire-watchers with us, but they were as anxious and willing and as efficient in their duties as were the male portion of the population. When the Fire Guard Organisation was officially set up Mr. W. G. Comfort, as Chief Warden, was responsible to the Council for the service, with Mr. S. H. Smith as Honorary Fire Guard Officer, but when it became necessary to appoint a full-time Fire Guard Officer, Mr. Smith was selected for the post. Much credit is due to him, his staff, and his volunteer assistants for the very satisfactory arrangements which were made to cover the Town in the event of a large incendiary raid, and for the action which they took when incendiaries actually fell in the area. Mr. Smith was subsequently awarded the British Empire Medal in recognition of his services.

The Assistance Board, whose offices were at Holm Lodge, London Road, found their hands full in dealing with victims of air raids after incidents had occurred. It was their duty to provide immediate financial assistance and clothing coupons to enable sufferers to purchase necessary clothing, etc., for their needs. The Citizens' Advice Bureau, too, led by Mrs. E. McCord, proved an invaluable amenity in assisting war victims to solve their difficulties.

Romford was happy in the possession of more than one Mobile Canteen. Two were lent to the Town for the period of the war without cost by the Ford Emergency Food Vans Trust. One was given outright to the Council by the Romford and District Chamber of Commerce, and a fourth was available from the Romford Branch of the W.V.S., who for the most part manned and drove the canteens, assisted sometimes by the Messenger Service. There was also an arrangement with Romford's Red Triangle Club for the use of the Y.M.C.A. tea vans if the necessity for, their use arose. To supplement these the British Restaurants functioned. These Restaurants, of which there were four, namely, at St. Andrew's Church Hall, the Hall of the Church of the Good Shepherd, Collier Row, at Victoria Road and at Rush Green Road, were under the supervision of Mrs. E. F. Carr, who, from their commencement until she left Romford in June, 1945, acted as Honorary Supervisor, assisted by Mrs. C. J. Hooton and a host of other ladies who were only too willing to give their services. There was, of course, a nucleus of paid workers at each Restaurant, and late at night and very early in the morning volunteers and paid workers gave their time in the cutting up of innumerable sandwiches and filling many urns with tea. The cafeteria sets never seemed to act as expeditiously as they might have done when the Mobile Canteens were waiting at the doors of the Restaurants to take refreshments to the scenes of incidents, but those refreshments got there very quickly, and such is the psychology of the average Britisher that a cup of tea and a sandwich went a long way to alleviate the pain which was felt when one knew that one's house and furniture had been destroyed, almost beyond replacement. It became quite a habit in the Report Centre to ask for a Mobile Canteen, and never once during the whole of the war period did the W.V.S. and the staffs at the Restaurants fail to answer a call for immediate assistance. In the same connection, the Romford Food Offic used to set up a temporary office for the distribution of emergency ration cards. It was most disheartening when one's small stock of rationed goods was destroyed by a bomb, and the assistance of one or two emergency ration cards to facilitate the purchase of a week or two's supply of rationed goods meant a lot to those people whose homes were damaged.

Again, there was the Emergency Information Officer of the Ministry of Information, whose loud-speaker van was helpful on many occasions in the making of various public announcements. The van appeared at incidents and gave people details of the various facilities which were at their disposal. Mr. A. J. Dyer was responsible for the service in Romford.

Lastly, we must remember the almost insuperable task which faced the Council in the repair of damaged houses and the demolition of those houses which were rendered dangerous. This work fell to the Borough Surveyor's Department, which, in the first instance, was called upon to remove to a place of safety such furniture and other belongings as could be retrieved from the damaged premises. When this was done the task was to render as many houses as possible habitable in the smallest space of time. The Borough Surveyor was assisted wholeheartedly by the builders in the town. He had a practice of telephoning during the night to the builders he needed, and it was the exception rather than the rule for the builders not to start on the repairs immediately it was light on the following morning. There were very few houses in Romford which were not damaged at all, and many letters of appreciation found their way to the Town Hall acknowledging the expeditious assistance of the Council in putting in hand the necessary repair to properties.

The foregoing is a brief and obviously inadequate review of the Civil Defence Services in Romford during the war. Mention of some organisation which did valuable work may have been omitted from this narrative and too much stress laid upon some particular branch of the Service, but the object of these notes is to give to the people of Romford some idea of the elaborateness of the Civil Defence Services as a whole, and at the same time to express appreciation of all that was seen of the Services in operation, throughout the whole of the period of the war.

THE SIRENS

Were located at the Town Hall; Messrs. Jessups' Garage, London Road; Police Station, Collier Row Lane; Plough Corner Police Station, Straight Road; The Brewery, High Street; and a hand siren was operated in Havering Village.

								Hrs.	Mins.
Sounded in 1939—	3 times, the " Alert " periods totalling							2	15
,,	,,	1940—417	,,	,,	,,	,,	,,	1,125	21½
,,	,,	1941—178	,,	,,	,,	,,	,,	309	52
,,	,,	1942— 32	,,	,,	,,	,,	,,	17	17
,,	,,	1943—111	,,	,,	,,	,,	,,	66	51
,,	;,	1944—469	,,	,,	,,	,,	,,	678	58
,,	,,	1945— 54	,,	,,	,,	,,	,,	10	35
In Total	1,264							2,211	9¼

The first " Alert " sounded at 11 a.m. on September 3rd, 1939.

The last " All Clear " sounded at 10.12 a.m. on March 29th, 1945.

The longest warning was from 18.43½ (25/10/40) to 07.02 (26/10/40), (12 hrs. 18¼ mins.).

The shortest warning was from 03.37 to 03.41 (27/3/45), (4 mins.).

The greatest number of " Alerts " in any 24 hours was 12 on July 21st, 1944.

The longest period under warning in any 24 hours was 16 hours 1½ minutes. This occurred on July 1st, 1944, and, in fact, at 12 midnight a warning was still in progress and continued until 6.53 in the morning of July 2nd, 1944.

41

STATISTICS

BOMBS, DAMAGE AND CASUALTIES

	1940	1941	1943	1944	1945	Total
High Explosive Bombs	344	78	6	8	—	436
Do. delayed action or unexploded ...	123	17	2	—	—	142
Oil Bombs, etc. (excluding small incendiaries)	58	—	—	—	—	58
TOTAL BOMBS ...	525	95	8	8	—	636
Parachute Mines ...	10	10	—	—	—	20
Do. (unexploded) ...	2	—	—	—	—	2
Fly Bombs	—	—	—	20	—	20
Long Range Rockets ...	—	—	—	8	13	21
Casualties—						
Fatalities	41	52	—	36	14	143
Hospital cases ...	56	66	1	124	22	269
Other casualties ...	108	86	1	243	78	516
	205	203	2	403	114	928

(NOTE.—Total population, 60,000 approximately)

	1940	1941	1943	1944	1945	Total
Damage—						
Properties demolished	136	152	1	152	31	472
,, seriously damaged	281	448	—	426	93	1,248
Others	9,144	4,839	293	10,840	3,147	28,263
TOTAL	9,561	5,439	294	11,418	3,271	29,983

(NOTE.—The total number of properties in Romford is approximately 18,000)

COMMENDATION

By MR. W. J. RUSSELL, O.B.E., J.P.

(County Sub-Controller of Civil Defence for Romford).

I commend this book to all Romfordians. It should find a place in every home, throughout the Borough, where its value and interest will increase as the years pass. It is part of Romford's history—a record of the manner in which the people of this Borough stood up to the enemy and looked after themselves, for that is what Civil Defence really means.

The physical and mental strain on everyone was great. The mother watching over her children, or, as was sometimes the case, having to hand them over to the care of others while she did her duty in the streets sharing danger equally with the men; the husband working at incidents, rescuing the trapped, tending the injured, and, when there was time to think, wondering whether his family was safe—these are but a few examples of tenacity and high courage.

The Heads of Services, with advance knowledge of possible new weapons and methods of attack, and always the responsibility of effectively minimising the effects of such attacks, had perpetually in mind the vital targets and possible combinations of damage which might put the town in major difficulties. Plans had to be ready for instant operation to deal with large numbers of homeless persons, rupture of communications, damage to or loss of C.D. personnel and vehicles, etc. All these things happened—indeed on one occasion it seemed they had all happened at once. These difficult situations were dealt with and we are all proud of those whose achievements were such that the C.D. Services received only high commendation from all and particularly from those who suffered personal loss, bereavement and damage to property.

Special congratulation must go to those who, occupying key positions in the Services, shared the strain and responsibility, as well as the danger, without thought of self. For myself, I could not have performed my task without the whole-hearted assistance of that small but efficient band of people and I gladly record my gratitude to them and to all members of the Civil Defence Service, for the assistance I received as a result of their loyalty and devotion to duty.

This record cannot be complete, for this would require a much larger book. Pathos in plenty, some grim humour and a degree of high courage beyond description which was found in all of Romford's citizens, made Romford's time of tribulation something of which all may be justly proud.

This book has told about Romford and its people and is one which I am sure all Romford people will desire to possess.

43

Romford Brewery, blasted by the same mine on December 8th, 1940.

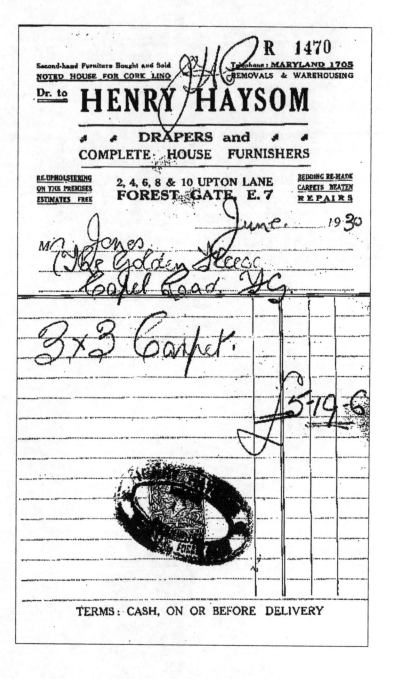

R 1470

Second-hand Furniture Bought and Sold
NOTED HOUSE FOR CORK LINO

Telephone: MARYLAND 1705
REMOVALS & WAREHOUSING

Dr. to

HENRY HAYSOM

❦ ❦ DRAPERS and ❦ ❦
COMPLETE HOUSE FURNISHERS

RE-UPHOLSTERING
ON THE PREMISES
ESTIMATES FREE

2, 4, 6, 8 & 10 UPTON LANE
FOREST GATE, E. 7

BEDDING RE-MADE
CARPETS BEATEN
REPAIRS

June. 1930

Mr Jones
The Golden Fleece
Capel Road. Yc

3 x 3 Carpet.   £5-19-6

TERMS: CASH, ON OR BEFORE DELIVERY

In the 1945 book all the photographs were in the last section. In this printing the pictures are scattered through the text. Pagination is unchanged and in this index pictures are in **bold type,** this indicating they are on a page opposite an original text page.